C000265278

The Alien Thing

Thing

Nowhere to Hide

And

Nowhere to Run

Anthony Fox

chipmunkapublishing
the mental health publisher

Published by
Chipmunkapublishing
United Kingdom

http://www.chipmunkapublishing.com

Cover Image Antonia Keen

Author of:
How to Pass a Degree with Confidence
It's Never Too Late
Babylon: The Gateway to the Gods
A Space Time Apocalypse
The Pirate Who Loved Me
The Truth Never Lies

Acknowledgements

I wish to thank my daughter Colleen and my son Jamie for their encouragement over the course of this book project.

Chapter 1

No one knew in the beginning what lay ahead for humanity. On the fertile plains of Mozambique, Africa the World Health Organisation (WHO) medical workers were busy trying to stem a possible outbreak of the recurring Ebola virus that had killed so many Africans over the years since it first emerged earlier in the century. It was a hot and sticky summer's day, in July, in a small village close to the Mozambique coastline when Harry Steel a Central Intelligence Agency (CIA) agent stood wondering where to start. He saw the main tent of the field hospital and decided he would make his way there and try to enlist some help. As he entered the tent and looked around, he could smell the stench of death, which lingered in the air, he thought.

"Who's in charge?" Harry Steel asked bluntly as he surveyed the scene inside the tent.

The African man turned around and pointed, "That's the doctor in charge!" Harry saw the doctor was flanked by a nurse on either side of him. He looked overworked and tired from the expression he could see on the doctor's sour face.

"Excuse me; I understand you're in charge here?" Harry asked as he winced at how hot it was inside the tent from the baking sun, which struck him as if hitting a brick wall.

"Yes, that's right. Who are you?" the doctor asked.

"My name is Harry Steel. I'm investigating the recent outbreak." This was partially true, but the CIA had other reasons to be interested in Africa.

"My name is Dr Oke Ben Tan most people just call me Dr Tan," the doctor said cheerfully. Continuing, he added, "You're very brave to walk in here. You do

4

know this is an Ebola clinic and all these patients you see are suspected to be infected with Ebola!"

"No shit!"

"Probably, only two months ago, I remember because it was my birthday. We had the first confirmed Ebola patient, exactly two months ago. Yes, two months to the day. He's over there recovering from the virus," the doctor said as he pointed to the corner of the tent.

"Oh, I see."

"Perhaps, we should talk outside…"

"Can you tell me when the outbreak started?" Harry asked as he followed the doctor outside and watched as the sweat dripped down from the doctor's face as if the sweat was in a race to the bottom of his chin.

"Is it the same strain of Ebola as of previous outbreaks?" Harry asked intently.

"Yes, I believe it is, but I haven't carried out those tests, other people in the WHO have done that analysis. You'd need to ask them." Dr. Tan winced and stressed what he believed and that he was not sure.

"Eh, so you're not sure, is that right?" Harry asked.

Dr. Tan grimaced and said, "Yes, that's right."

"How high is the mortality rate?"

"Not as high as previous outbreaks when the mortality rate was around eighty per cent and this time it has dropped to around thirty per cent, but we're getting better at saving lives as we learn more. We have better drugs and treatments," Dr. Tan replied.

"Yeah, it's a lot better, what about drugs…what therapeutics are you using?" Harry asked intently. Harry could be blunt some times that was his youth talking and his background growing up in Brooklyn.

"Remdesivir has saved a lot of lives. And there's

a new drug that the WHO is trialling at the moment called Dexamethasone. Combined with the right amount of hydration patients with the virus have a good chance of recovery, provided they don't have underlying health issues."

"Yes, I understand. One final question, how many of the population do you suspect have the virus?" Harry asked.

Shrugging his shoulders the doctor replied, "Currently, we're not sure, but the virus is spreading at an exponential rate. Either, from droplets in the air or through bodily contact these are the two ways you can contract the virus."

The CIA had sent Harry Steel to find out what was happening in Mozambique with the Ebola outbreaks and not to expose the truth to the world, which the CIA could not allow to happen. From the outside, the CIA would seem to be callous in their approach to the truth. It was not about the welfare of the Ebola patients or the drugs being used that concerned the CIA, but something far bigger than even national security and they wanted to keep it that way for as long as possible.

Harry said his thanks to Dr Tan, and then made his way back to his parked Ford SUV on the outskirts of the village where a group of children were merrily playing near his vehicle. It would be an hour's journey back to the capital Maputo before he arrived back at the hotel with time enough to reflect on his mission. He had been given the file for the mission by his friend and boss; Michael Kurios Director of Counter Intelligence at the CIA headquarters in Langley, Virginia the USA before boarding the corporate Learjet at Norfolk International Airport. Harry's boss had been explicit in his orders, do whatever you need to do to keep the truth from going public. Whatever the truth was Harry would do his best to keep it a secret, he said to himself.

Harry Steel relished the mission and saw with his warm brown eyes as he surveyed the scene like any other over his career in the CIA, but this mission had all hallmarks of being his last, even though he had over ten more years to go before his official retirement age, he said to himself. He grimaced at the prospect of retirement but he did not fear death. He had reconciled the chance of catching a bullet and often said to colleagues that worrying about it would not stop a bullet. No, the prospect of retirement really worried him, he said to himself. He was still lean, fit and with a mop of greyish black wavy hair still had his Italian looks, but did not have any plans for his retirement and no hobbies other than watching the river that gently meandered its way past his country cabin in the foothills of the Appalachian Mountains. When he had the time, he would sit on the embankment and read and watch the river flow by and gaze at the fish making their presence felt as a ripple, on the surface, in the almost still waters of the slowly moving river.

Chapter 2

Meanwhile, inside the Kremlin, the Russian President was sat waiting for Alexi Polokov his newly promoted Chief of the Intelligence Secret Service to arrive. Alexi Polokov was in his mid-forties and a former Spetsnaz officer and a family man with a wife and three children and a devoted communist party member above all else. He had the latest news of its cooperation with the Americans concerning the mission code-named Iceberg. The president of Russia had stayed in power for nearly two decades since changing the Russian constitution to allow for continuous re-elections in his favour. It was a kind of democracy with a Russian twist. The cooperation with the Americans was a state secret and had been for a considerable time and they wanted to keep it that way. The public did not need to know why there was open hostility between the two nations, which was well known and expected by their populations. At the highest echelons of power it was necessary to have an ever-present enemy, so higher and higher budgets could be secured for military purposes. But, behind the charade, they shared the same bed. All their efforts had been to quietly bring their military forces up to the level of the new enemy, without alarming the population. They wanted the average Joe to continue paying his bills and for their kids to go to school. They wanted a contented population while they figured out how to match the new enemy that threatened the world with its very existence.

"We have sent an agent to assist the Americans in Mozambique," Alexi Polokov Chief of the Intelligence Secret Service said.

"What agent comrade?" the president asked snappily.

"Agent Dr. Olga Domleic," Alexi replied matter-of-factly.

"What news of Mozambique?" the president asked intensely.

"It's a mess!" Pausing, to see the reaction on the face of the president, Alexi continued, and he added, "There've been Ebola outbreaks all over the country and the WHO are at present trying to contain the virus before it spreads to other countries. I understand the CIA has been busy trying to figure out the cause because it seems suspicious to them," Alexi replied.

"What do you think comrade?" the president asked sharply.

"Our intelligence suggests that it looks suspicious that's why we're sending in our agent to assist the Americans, we want to know the truth," Alexi said dutifully.

"When will our agent arrive on the scene comrade?" the president asked.

"She's already on an aeroplane and should arrive early tomorrow morning. We'll know more when she sends in her first report later that day," Alexi replied.

***

On the flight to Mozambique, Dr. Olga Domleic was seated with other Russian military personnel on the Antonov An-148 cargo plane, which gave her the time to study the file she had been given by Sergey Kovic the deputy to the Chief of the Russian Intelligence Service when she was assigned to the mission. The file was labelled: Top Secret, but that was no surprise to Olga as most missions were secret and this mission was no different. At all costs, the public was not to know anything about the mission the file stressed. The file was sketchy about facts. All that was known was that a series of Ebola outbreaks had occurred in suspicious circumstances all around Mozambique and the Russian Intelligence Service wanted to know why. Olga had been told to liaise with a CIA agent in Mozambique and to make reports daily back to Russia.

Olga thought it was strange that she had been told to assist the Americans when usually they were on opposite sides of the cloak and dagger world of espionage. But, she guessed there were good reasons for the collaboration; otherwise, her boss would have not made a point of tasking her to assist the CIA. Reading on, she realised there was a pattern to the Ebola outbreaks, but she could not put her finger on it, at that moment, she said to herself. The saving grace was the lower mortality rate compared to earlier outbreaks in other African countries, in previous years. Yet, she could see a pattern and wondered why the WHO had not seen the same; perhaps they had and had chosen to keep that a secret from the public, she said to herself.

***

On the drive from the airport towards the village where the latest Ebola outbreak had occurred, she wondered if the CIA agent would still be about. She had a mobile number to contact, which was in the file and had sent a message to the phone before leaving the airport. She was curious and eager to meet the CIA agent and to start working together. It was then that she heard her mobile ringing as she then pulled off the road and answered the phone call.

"Hello, I received your message, my name is Harry Steel," Harry said.

"Yes, my name is Dr Olga Domleic. I understand we're working together on this case, where are you now?" Olga asked politely.

"I'm on my way to meet you at the village,"

Harry replied. Continuing, he added, "Be there in thirty minutes, see you then." And he abruptly ended the call.

Harry Steel, she said to herself. It was a name she could recall reading about in intelligence reports she had previously studied. She had not met the CIA man before but hoped it would be a fruitful relationship. She noticed the village was not much to write home about. Most of the homes were just corrugated shacks with some built with reed roofs and mud-brick walls. She saw an African man dressed in white and figured it to be a doctor.

"Hello, are you in charge here?"

"Yes, my name is Dr Tan."

"Right, my name is Dr Olga Domleic. I need to ask a few questions about the Ebola outbreak."

"You're not the first person today to ask such questions," Dr. Tan replied. Continuing, he added, "You have an accent, where are you from?"

"I'm from Russia, my government which helps support your country is trying to understand as much as possible about the Ebola outbreaks. It has already set up quarantine areas for its citizens and military personnel that arrive back in Russia from here. It's worried that the virus may spread into its population. When did the outbreak occur in this village?"

"Two months ago, today," Dr. Tan replied.

"Oh, I see. What about treatments?" Olga asked.

"We're using Remdesivir and trialling a new drug called Dexamethasone. Both of these drugs have reduced the mortality rate from previous outbreaks to thirty per cent from around eighty per cent," Dr. Tan said.

"How's the virus spreading?"

"There're two main ways from air droplets and person to person contact. So, you need to be careful whom you talk to and what you touch," Dr. Tan replied.

Continuing, he added, "Did you hear that loud monkey or lemur calling its mate, just then…?"

"Yeah, it's loud enough to get noticed out here, in the jungle," Olga remarked.

"There goes another calling its mate…"

"That got the birds squawking; now they're making their presence felt…"

"And the background constant buzz of millions of insects adding to the experience," Dr. Tan said.

"Okay, doctor that's all I need to know, for now, thanks for your help," Olga said. Continuing, she added, "Oh, have you seen a pattern in the outbreaks?"

Shaking his head, Dr. Tan replied briskly, "No, I haven't seen one!"

Olga found it odd that the doctor had not seen a pattern to the outbreaks, but figured it may be due to how busy he was with the outbreak he was dealing with. As she waited for the CIA agent to arrive she walked around the village and wondered why Ebola had struck only in Africa and no other part of the world. She was not an expert, but she had seen a pattern in the outbreaks, she said to herself.

"Hello, my name is Dr. Olga Domleic and you?"

"Harry Steel. I interviewed the doctor earlier today. I don't have much information to share with you."

"That's alright; I've already spoken to the doctor and have the same answers he gave you. But have you seen the pattern in the outbreaks?" Olga asked intently.

Shrugging his shoulders, Harry replied, "No, what do you mean?"

"Well, a pattern in the outbreaks."

"A pattern I've yet to see," Harry said in disbelief.

"Yeah, a pattern, you can see it, if you stand outside the box. Consider this: Don't you think it's odd that a deadly virus, which is highly contagious, has spread its wings all over Mozambique, yet it's failed to appear in another neighbouring country in Africa. And then there's the vexed question of why the virus hasn't spread itself around the world," Olga said.

"No, I haven't thought about it too deeply. But, I did wonder why I'd been put on this mission. But, it looks like you're on to something. At least, we now have two heads working on the mission."

"Oh, I see…"

"Did you ask the doctor about possible patterns?" Harry asked.

"Yes, he said, he saw no pattern. But, I figured he was too busy dealing with the current outbreak in this village to notice a pattern."

"Perhaps, he knows more but is keeping it quiet."

"Perhaps, but I'm not sure. Don't you think it's odd our two countries are working together?" Olga asked intently.

"I don't think that far. In the meantime, where are you staying at?" Harry asked.

"I've booked into the Aerotel Hotel and you?"

"Snap! The same hotel…good, we can get to know each other and share information easily." Harry replied, smiling.

Olga half smiled back at Harry. She was not in the mood to play games and any relationship would be purely business. She thought Harry was probably going through a mid-life crisis that he had not personally recognised yet. She felt it would be up to her to keep him on the straight and narrow and for him to forget about her female charms, she said to herself.

"Let's meet later in the hotel bar and exchange information."

"Yes, sounds like a plan," Olga replied, smiling.

She wanted the business relationship to work, but was not prepared to play second fiddle to his manly advances.

"In the meantime, I need to get back and write my report, short and sweet," Harry said, smiling. He also wanted to get back to the hotel and do some checking up on the Russian agent before he got too deeply involved with her. He wanted to know as much information on her background before he committed fully to the joint working relationship.

Olga immediately noticed Harry's candour and smiled again and felt the mission was at least intriguing on two fronts. The odd pattern that she could see and Harry's way with words would keep her on her toes, she said to herself.

"Yes, a few Vodkas will help with the heat in my throat!"

"Yeah, a few JDs and cokes will go down well after this humid air," Harry said. At that moment, he felt the dryness at the back of his throat as if something had sucked all the moisture from his mouth.

"On the way back, I'll reflect on what you said about the pattern and look forward to my drinks tonight, and of course seeing you there." Harry was intrigued to find out what the Russian agent was thinking and was looking forward to having a drink with the tall and beautiful blue-eyed blond. Suddenly, Harry and Olga heard a loud roar emanating from the surrounding jungle and they both wondered what it was.

As Harry made his way to his vehicle and drove off thinking about his next move, he wondered if Olga was right, and if there was a pattern then his next move would be to see what the WHO thought about the Ebola outbreaks. As he passed palm plantations neatly replacing tropical forests that had been ecologically virgin to such devastation, he reflected, on climate change and the Ebola outbreaks. Could they be connected in some way? The question rattled around his mind, but he could not find an answer. At least, an answer that satisfied his logical thinking mind, he said to himself. Olga was right about Mozambique's air, he thought. At times, it was like sucking in a hot pipe of air into your lungs, you felt the hot air all the way down. The only saving grace was the prospect of a cold drink to soothe the throat from the heat and the dust, later that night, he said to himself.

***

On the way back to the hotel, Olga reflected on her meeting with Harry Steel, Dr. Tan and the Ebola crisis. She passed palm plantations as far as the eye could see and realised the topography of Mozambique had changed dramatically. Was it related to the Ebola outbreak, she was not sure, she said to herself? She would have to do some more research back at the hotel. Her employers wanted an in-depth investigation into the Ebola outbreak, which had intrigued her because she was a highly trained agent, not an epidemiologist. The cooperation between Russia and America in this case caused alarm bells to ring in her head because it was a first for her. And she felt Dr. Tan was elusive and probably knew more. And that Harry Steel was also a character who was just as elusive as a black cat on a moonless night, she thought.

***

Back at the hotel, Harry and Olga met up at the hotel's bar for a few drinks and discussed the mission. They both had their own views on the Ebola outbreaks, which neither one was willing to let go of at that particular moment in time.

"What's your drink?"

"Vodka and soda, please," Olga replied.

Harry ordered the drinks at the hotel bar and carefully watched the other customers in the room.

"What are your thoughts about today?" Olga asked.

"Ummm, let me see." Harry took another sip of his JK and coke before giving his answer. He was in no rush; he was full of contemplation on the whole mission, which did not fit with his normal role as a CIA spy, he thought. The CIA had sent him to Mozambique to find the answers to the questions they probably already feared. There was something fishy about the mission he could almost taste it, he said to himself. He felt his friend and boss Michael Kurios had been reluctant to tell him the full truth, which caused him to fear the worst. He did not like being put in the firing line without knowing what was going on, he said to himself.

"What's the WHO doing in Mozambique?" Olga asked intently.

"Not a lot, in some respects, similar, to their failure at the beginning of the Covid-19 crisis, a few years ago, when they failed to call it a pandemic when it needed that leadership call. We all know how the American president felt about the WHO often referring to the WHO as an organisation, which wasn't fit for purpose. I have a meeting with the top honcho in Mozambique tomorrow morning; it is best if you tag along as well as we're supposed to be working together," Harry said.

"Yes, you're right. Let's see what they say tomorrow. In the meantime, I need a few more Vodkas."

"What you said about a pattern is a big clue to this Ebola outbreak and the reason why two spies are now on the case." Harry felt the Russian agent was on to something but was not willing to say too much about her theory that there was a pattern in the Ebola outbreaks, it niggled him, as he was eager to know more.

Chapter 3

It was a hot and humid morning, in late July, on the drive through the capital city of Maputo to the WHO headquarters in Mozambique. Harry Steel and Dr. Olga Domleic had decided to start early that morning as their employers had wanted results as fast as possible. The Ebola outbreaks in Mozambique had been unexpected and yet they revealed a pattern, which Olga had noticed right from the beginning and Harry had tagged along with. They both felt it odd that Dr. Tan had not noticed the pattern, and both felt the doctor knew more than he was willing to admit to.

"I'm Dr. Phillip Fellows and head of day to day operations here for the WHO."

"Good morning," Harry and Olga said to the head of operations.

"Good morning. Why are you here?" the head of operations asked.

"My name is Harry Steel and this is my colleague Dr. Olga Domleic. We're here to ask what the WHO is doing about the Ebola crisis in the country."

"As you may know we have Ebola outbreaks throughout the country. And our mission is to assist the Mozambique government in its efforts to control the outbreaks and see to it that the outbreaks are kept under control. I understand you spoke with Dr. Tan yesterday, in our most recent outbreak, in the small village just outside the capital?" Dr. Fellows said.

"Yes, that's correct," Harry said and Olga nodded her head in agreement.

"Have you noticed the pattern of the outbreaks?" Olga asked hurriedly and was not willing to wait for Harry to ask another question.

"What pattern, I've seen no pattern?" Dr.

Fellows replied strenuously.

"The pattern is clearly visible to me and should be to you," Olga said sharply. She watched the face of the operations director to see if it revealed any signs of misgivings.

Shrugging his shoulders and shaking his head, Dr. Fellows said, "No, I see no pattern, explain the pattern." The doctor felt under pressure from the questioning of Olga and Harry.

"You've had outbreaks all over Mozambique, but in small villages and not in any major towns or cities, why is that?" Olga persisted.

"Yes, why is that?" Harry grimaced and asked again.

"It's because of our efforts to keep the virus under control by controlling the population in the villages and not allowing it to spread to towns and cities. Plus, in these small villages, they have little idea about hand hygiene and basic sanitation. This is why the outbreaks have occurred in villages and not in the cities," Dr. Fellows replied and felt he had answered their questions succinctly and truthfully.

Olga felt it was a reasonable answer, but too convenient a reply from the doctor. She felt the doctor was not telling the truth and the WHO was holding back the truth for some reason. She continued to press the doctor for more answers.

"When do you think you will have the Ebola crisis fully under control?" Harry asked.

"How long is a piece of string? To be frank with you…we don't know. It all depends on the infection rate. When we see that coming down and providing we don't have another outbreak in the meantime, we won't know for sure if we have controlled the virus," Dr. Fellows replied, smiling. Harry and Olga both noticed the smirk across the doctor's face and felt it was not warranted.

"Is it the same Ebola virus that has struck other countries in Africa previously?" Olga asked intently.

"You mean the same strain? Well, yes it's just mutated as normal," Dr. Fellows replied. Continuing, he added, "Each virus will mutate in the course of its existence. Sometimes these small mutations make the virus more virulent or less so. It can be the smallest change that could make the biggest difference in how the virus behaves," Dr. Fellows replied.

"So, it's the same virus as far as you can tell?" Olga asked.

"Yes."

Dr. Fellows explained that Deoxyribonucleic acid (DNA) was a molecule composed of two chains that coil around each other to form a double helix carrying genetic instructions for the reproduction of that organism.

"Each time the virus enters a cell in a patient it copies its DNA into that cell, but occasionally it doesn't copy exactly the same copy of itself. It loses some of the DNA in the copying process and that's how it mutates over time," Dr. Fellows explained. Continuing, he added, "Essentially, it's a bit more complicated than that, but that's the nuts and bolts of the process."

"So, you see no pattern emerging is that right?" Harry asked intently. Harry felt he needed to ask the same question again.

"No, as I said before there's no pattern, otherwise, we would've seen it long before now, believe me," Dr. Fellows replied. Continuing, he added, "If there was a pattern we would've been on to it like a dog on heat."

"Is there any reason why the Ebola crisis started in Mozambique?" Olga asked intently.

"I don't have an answer. We just don't know why an outbreak occurs here and not somewhere else. It's not something we spend time thinking about. The WHO gets called in when the situation gets out of control and the government asks us to help them deal with the emergency. We believe the Ebola virus comes from fruit bats, which the locals in the small villages prey on for food. The fruit bat carries hundreds of viruses and it probably jumped from the bat to humans much like a common cold," Dr. Fellows replied. Continuing, he added, "You have to remember that bats are closely related to humans on the evolutionary tree. So, it makes sense that a bat can easily transfer its viruses to humans, especially when they're being cut up and made ready to cook. Any blood transferred to the human by way of the hand to mouth is enough to start the process."

"Well, that's it, for now, we may be in touch later if we need help," Harry said. Continuing, he added, "Unless you have more questions for the doctor, Olga?"

"Yes, just one, can you point us to another outbreak that we can visit, today," Olga asked.

"Yes, of course, it's just outside the capital close to the copper mines. It's again a small village called Lusa, you need to follow the main road south along the coastline and then into the bush before you reach the copper mines. I believe it's signposted if you have a Satnav," Dr. Fellows replied.

"Yes, thanks for your help and time," Harry said and Olga affirmed by nodding her head. As Harry and Olga thanked the doctor and made their way out of the WHO headquarters they both still had their doubts about what the WHO was doing in Mozambique. But, not satisfied they headed south in Harry's rented SUV vehicle out of the capital towards the village with a current outbreak of Ebola, near the copper mines, which the doctor had talked about. The air conditioning in the car was on full blast and keeping the heat of the mid-day sun from melting their will to find the truth.

"What did you think about Dr Fellows?" Harry asked Olga as he tried to concentrate on the road traffic. He wanted to see if she had the same kind of doubts he had in his mind. He felt the whole mission was suspicious and not the usual mission for a spy. And also the vexed question of why his boss felt he needed help from the Russians. He was well aware of the Russian and American cooperation in space, but apart from that, they were usually enemies. Harry knew he would normally perform better when his judgement was not clouded by an opposing adversary right on his shoulder, even though she was a beautiful woman to look at. But, he was willing to toe the line for now, until he figured out what was going on because he felt his boss had not told him the full story, he said to himself.

"I felt the doctor wasn't telling the full story, but that's my gut instinct talking. I don't have any proof for my doubts, just a feeling," Olga replied. Continuing, she added, "And what about you, do you feel the same?" She looked across at Harry's face for a reaction and saw him wince before replying.

"Yes, I've had my doubts on just about everything on this mission so far, but perhaps we will know more when we visit this village, today," Harry replied. Continuing, he added, "Look, more palm plantations!" As far as the eye could see on both sides of the road far into the distance the jungle had been cut down for the palm plantations.

"Yeah, the country's ecology is changing fast and without understanding the ramifications, I expect," Olga said. At that moment, the Satnav spoke and told them to make a right turn off the main highway onto a dirt track leading into what was remaining of the bush below the mountains.

For several miles, Harry and Olga saw only the bush, forest and jungle along the dirt track, without coming across any people. They noticed the terrain change from rolling plains to the thick jungle, in the shadow of the mountain peaks, as their vehicle slowly climbed to the lower levels of the jungle-covered mountain range. After driving an hour, on the dirt track, Harry and Olga could see the reed-covered and corrugated roofs of homes, in the distance, and people milling about as their vehicle slowly descended to the outskirts of the village. On reaching the village they parked and saw the WHO field tent and made their way on foot to find the person in charge.

"Hello, who's in charge here?" Harry asked the young man dressed in a white hazmat suit.

"Dr Kembe is inside the tent," the young man said. Continuing, he added, "But, I wouldn't go in there unless you are dressed correctly."

Harry grimaced at the words from the young man and looked at Olga for her reaction. She also winced at the thought of entering the tent.

"Listen, can you ask Dr Kembe we're here from America and Russia to discuss the outbreak," Harry stressed to the young man.

"I didn't know what else to say," Harry said as they waited outside for the doctor to appear. It was several minutes before Dr. Kembe appeared fully dressed in a hazmat suit with a respirator and Harry and Olga watched as the doctor was then cleaned by colleagues and helped to undress out of the hazmat suit.

"Hello, my name is Harry Steel and this is my colleague Dr. Olga Domleic, we spoke with Dr. Fellows at WHO headquarters in Maputo this morning," Harry

said.

"Hi, my name is Dr. Kembe, how can I help?" Dr. Kembe asked mystified.

"Just a few questions about the Ebola outbreak, have you noticed any patterns to the outbreaks across the country?" Olga asked who was eager to get going and get the hell out of the place as soon as possible.

"Patterns, no, I can't say I have, but then I haven't had the time to look at other outbreaks," Dr. Kembe replied. Continuing, he added, "Is there one?"

"Well, that's what we're here to find out," Harry replied.

"What's the mortality rate and what drugs are you using to combat the virus?" Olga asked.

"The mortality rate is around thirty per cent and we use Remdesivir and Dexamethasone to combat the virus. These drugs make a big difference to a person's chance of surviving the infection. Without these drugs, the mortality rate would be nearer eighty per cent," Dr. Kembe stressed.

"You have no problems obtaining these drugs then?" Harry asked.

"No, we've plenty of supplies."

"Do you know how the outbreak started?" Olga asked.

"We're not sure; we think it may have come here through another carrier. But, like I said we're not sure," Dr. Kembe replied.

"When you say we, who do you mean?" Harry asked.

"I mean the WHO."

"How's the virus spread?" Olga asked.

"Through bodily fluids, air droplets and person to person contact. It's highly contagious, that's why you saw me fully protected by a hazmat suit and respirator,"

Dr. Kembe replied.

"Yes, that's why we didn't want to go into your field hospital tent," Harry remarked.

"How long does it normally take to recover from the virus?" Olga asked.

"It all depends on the patient, but around two months if there're no underlying health issues."

"Is there a reason why major towns and cities haven't seen outbreaks?" Harry asked.

"Yes, it's because we quarantine the village and stop all contact with the outside world. It's as simple as that!" Dr. Kembe replied.

"Well, thanks for your help and time," Harry said and Olga thanked the doctor separately.

"Oh, almost forgot, why is it that at the other outbreak we saw yesterday we saw no one wearing hazmat suits, yet, you were wearing them here?" Olga asked.

"That's because we're at an early stage in the outbreak with people still coming in with the virus. Most likely at the other outbreak, they're at a later stage…the recovery stage when patients aren't infectious," Dr. Kembe replied.

"Well, thanks again, we'll be on our way back."

On the drive back to the capital, Harry and Olga discussed what they thought. Olga again stressed she had her suspicions about the mission as did Harry. Olga could not put her finger on it and nor could Harry, both thought something was amiss.

"Perhaps, we need to see another outbreak," Harry suggested.

"One where we pick the outbreak," Olga suggested.

"We'll check out the Internet later and do our own search and see what we can find," Harry said.

"In the meantime, I fancy stopping at a highway service centre and getting something to eat, while we're out this way what say you?" Olga asked politely.

"Yes, that's a good idea. Always good to try out the local food," Harry replied, smiling. Continuing, he added, "As soon as I see a place I'll stop."

"What did you think about Dr Kembe?" Olga asked.

"He sounded genuine to me, but then again I'm not a doctor. So, it's difficult to be sure. That's why I don't think my employers have told me the complete truth about this mission. I have had my suspicions since the start. What about you?"

"My brief was the same as yours. Come out here and find out what is going on with the Ebola crisis and report back as soon as possible. I don't think they've told me the complete truth, as well. I have had my suspicions from the start as you did," Olga replied.

"That was a long drive out of the jungle and now we're on the main highway we should see a rest stop any time soon," Harry said.

"Look! Just miles and miles of nothing but palm plantations on both sides of the highway, and stretching right up to the edge of the mountains in the distance," Olga said.

"What do they use these palm plantations for?" Harry asked.

"Everything you can imagine, from makeup products to food supplements. They use the oil from the palm plant as a base oil to mix with more exotic oils that are scarcer. I believe it takes about two years before they can harvest the palm oil from the plant. It's a big cash crop for the country. But, the downside is the destruction of virgin jungle and forests that are gone forever," Olga replied.

"I guess that's progress, it could be part of the reason why these Ebola outbreaks have occurred. I remember, reading how E.coli one five seven was spread by cow droppings in fields with apple orchards. Children would pick up fallen apples off the ground where the cows had been and then they inadvertently contracted the disease. And there's no cure," Harry said regretfully.

"E.coli one five seven?"

"Yes, it's a deadly disease to humans, but lives in the guts of cows quite happily," Harry said.

"You're a world of wisdom, Harry," Olga said, laughing.

"I don't know about that, but when I get the time I read all kinds of stuff. I guess it's the only hobby I have. What about you…what do you do for relaxation?" Harry asked.

"Sailing!"

"Not another one," Harry said, smiling.

"What do you mean, Harry?"

"It doesn't matter, just a previous mission. I won't go into that," Harry said, laughing.

Harry saw the rest stop and pulled into the car park off the highway. Harry and Olga both noticed how busy the rest stop was and they were relieved to take a break. They soon felt the hot air outside choking at their throats as they walked the short distance into the rest stop. And they also noticed the clouds of dust blowing from the direction of the open-air copper mine, which Dr. Fellows had mentioned.

Harry grimaced at the sour taste in his throat and wondered if it was the copper mine. Olga had a similar experience but winced at the dust blowing into her face. Her sunglasses had stopped most of the dust, but not all of it blowing into her eyes. She immediately felt a burning sensation around her eyes that were already weeping. She immediately headed for the restroom to wash out her eyes.

After washing his hands in the restroom, Harry found an empty table and sat down and waited for Olga to return from the restroom. It was hot and sticky inside the rest stop with only a few ceiling fans whirling around trying to keep the place cool. It was not like America where air conditioning reigned supreme everywhere you went, he said to himself.

Now in his late forties, he had spent most of his adult life protecting the American dream one way or another, since leaving university with a degree in politics from the University of California, Los Angeles (UCLA) and then he had served as a Marine in the second Gulf war and for the last twenty years or so in the CIA. He often said that one half of the world at any given time was trying to join the American dream and the other half trying to destroy America, he thought.

"Your eyes look sore."

"Yes, it was that damn dust outside."

"Can I take your order?" the waitress asked.

After ordering their drinks and meals, Harry wanted to see if Olga had any observations about their previous visit. He felt suspicious about the previous doctor and wanted to touch base with Olga to see if she felt the same. At the same time, he continued to watch the only entrance to the rest stop for any suspicious characters. His training had taught him never to be too relaxed. He wanted to know if they were being followed.

"I have my suspicions about Dr Kembe," Harry said.

"Yes, you said before and I feel the same," Olga said.

"It could be fraud on the part of the WHO," Harry said. Continuing, he added, "I don't know who's involved, but it stinks!"

"What are our plans for the rest of today?" Olga asked.

"Well, get back to the hotel and get on the Internet and do some searching. We need to find another recent outbreak," Harry suggested. Continuing, he added, "Hopefully, we can see it today."

"Yes, I agree."

"How are your eyes, Olga?"

"Still sore, but still able to see!" Olga replied nonchalantly.

"Here are your meals and drinks," the waitress said as she placed them on the table.

"Thanks."

"I may call in a local CIA asset to help us research the WHO in Mozambique," Harry suggested.

"Is that wise, considering how secret this mission is meant to be," Olga said.

"Yes and no, but it may need the local expertise to unravel the mystery. I won't tell the asset if you don't," Harry said, smiling.

"Now, you're just being cavalier like a jester at court," Olga said, smiling.

"Seriously, I'm good at finding a rat, but I'm no doctor when it comes to understanding the ins and outs of an Ebola outbreak, so an outside expert may be the answer. My brief was to find out what was going on here and report back tout suite," Harry said nonchalantly.

"If it's a fraud like you suspect then we'll soon find out soon enough," Olga said. Continuing, she added, "My theory is the pattern like I said before. There's a pattern and there shouldn't be one!"

"Oh, by the way, what are you a doctor of?" Harry asked cheekily.

"Yes, I should've said before. I'm a biologist,"

Olga replied.

"Tell me more…what does a biologist do?"

"I qualified as a biologist but haven't done any out in the field of real-world biology. Soon after I qualified I joined the secret service," Olga replied.

"Yes, but what does a biologist actually do?"

"Right, it's the study of organisms, plants and animals and how they work under environmental conditions such as climate change. I originally wanted to help improve the genetics of crops for better food production. It's a big subject so many specialise in a particular aspect of biology. I got side-tracked and as I said before I joined the secret service," Olga replied.

"Oh, I see."

"And while we're on the subject what about you?" Olga asked intently.

"Not much to say. I studied politics at university and haven't looked back since," Harry replied, smiling. He did not feel the need to elaborate on his past and besides she could check his file back in Russia if she wanted a breakdown of his skills, he said to himself. Continuing, he added, "Changing the subject, do you still feel there's a pattern to the Ebola outbreaks?"

"Yes, I do, it's the thing I feel totally sure of right now," Olga replied briskly.

"Hmm, I understand…"

"Do you?"

"Well, I understand your reasoning about the pattern, but we were told the reasons why there's no pattern to the Ebola outbreaks. So, unless we've been told a bunch of lies then there's something else going on like a massive fraud by the WHO," Harry replied.

Olga just winced at Harry's remarks and watched his facial expressions. As Harry watched the comings and goings of the rest stop as he ate his meal his training as a CIA agent told him to be cautious wherever he went. He watched every person looking for a person or persons that looked out of place. He wanted to be sure he and Olga were not being followed. It was standard practice to always be on the lookout as a CIA agent and today was no different from any other day, he said to himself.

"Are we being followed, Harry," Olga asked. Continuing she added, "I've seen you watching the front door ever since I sat down."

"No, not so far, but I'm still looking!"

"What makes you think it's a massive fraud by the WHO?" Olga asked intently.

"It's just a theory, but at any time it could change governed by the facts. I'm prepared always to change my viewpoint depending on new evidence, but at the moment, I believe there's some sort of fraud going on. Now, it could be local or have a much larger footprint consisting of the whole organisation or some part of it. We all know that money corrupts and in this business and from my experience I've learned never to be surprised. As a CIA agent, it pays never to be surprised…you live longer," Harry said nonchalantly.

"You didn't answer the question!" Olga asked intently.

"I thought I did…"

"You didn't give your reasons, why you thought it was a massive fraud!" Olga asked again.

"The same answer, I just did, were you not listening!"

Olga winced at his reply and smiled back, "Okay, I give in."

"Simple, Simon, says put your hand on your head and let's get the hell out of here," Harry said, laughing.

Back in their car heading towards the hotel they continued their conversation.

"Seriously, the reasons are varied, but when we have seen an outbreak that someone else hasn't guided us there, I will know more," Harry said.

"So, you don't have any reasons why it's a fraud," Olga persisted.

"If I told you now it wouldn't be a surprise!"

"We're meant to be sharing information that's the point of partners," Olga said irksomely.

"Partners, I didn't think you thought that way about us!" Harry said, smiling. Continuing, he added, "But, it's interesting."

Harry was not sure who would be right and he felt it was better for Olga to not cloud her mind with his theory. He would outline his reasons when the time was right. It was better they had independent views at this point in their investigation rather than fly with one flag. Harry knew that money corrupts and it was rife in Africa.

"Look!" Harry pointed to the people walking the streets of the capital as they crisscrossed the city to the hotel. "Most citizens don't have a dime to stand on or let alone to spend. It doesn't take much to corrupt some people."

"Aren't you being cynical?" Olga asked.

"No, just pointing out the truth!"

"Really, I don't see how."

"I will know more when we've visited another outbreak!"

Harry soon found another outbreak on his Internet search at the hotel and was pleased it was only a few hours' drive away. As Harry and Olga made their way to the village they saw a summer's mist had formed along the coastline partially obscuring the sun's rays as it sprinkled an array of light like twinkling stars in the universe upon the sea.

***

On the journey to the Ebola outbreak, they discussed their tactics and decided they would approach the interviewing differently and they decided it should only be from Olga unless Harry decided to intervene.

"At least, the landscape is different," Harry remarked.

On the journey, the traffic along the highway started to disperse the closer they got to their target village. As they turned off the highway and into the bush they drove along a dirt track that led into the jungle. After nearly an hour on the dirt track, they saw the outskirts of the village emerge from the jungle. Harry and Olga then saw the white hospital tent pitched away from the village buildings and parked their vehicle and made their way there by foot.

"Who's in charge here?" Harry asked the old man sat down on a nearby bench.

"The doctor...Dr. Hamas inside...," the old man replied pointing to the tent.

Harry was not sure about entering the tent without the need for the proper protection.

"Hello, hello...Dr Hamas," Harry shouted out hoping they could hear him inside the tent. After a few minutes, an African man appeared dressed in white.

"I'm Dr Hamas...how can I help?" Dr. Hamas asked.

"My name is Harry Steel and this is Dr Olga Domleic. We would like to ask a few questions about the Ebola outbreak," Harry said.

"When did it start?" Olga asked.

"About two months ago," Dr. Hamas replied. Continuing, he added, "We haven't had a new patient with the virus for three weeks."

"You believe you have dealt with the problem?" Olga stressed.

"Yes, we saved a lot of people. With the new drugs…we have saved lives," Dr. Hamas said.

"What drugs are you using on the patients?"

"We use Remdesivir and a new drug called Dexamethasone, which has brought the mortality rate down to around thirty per cent. In other Ebola outbreaks in Africa, we saw mortality rates at nearer eighty per cent," Dr. Hamas said cheerfully.

Chapter 4

Meanwhile, at the CIA headquarters at Langley, Virginia, in America, on the third floor, inside a secure room free from all electronic bugging devices sat Michael Kurios Director of Counter Intelligence with all the other section directors and the overall director Paul Henderson who had direct access to the president of the United States of America. The CIA was split into six separate divisions, which ranged from counter-intelligence to internal affairs.

"I convened this meeting today to discuss the present problem of keeping the truth about our enemy away from the public," Paul Henderson CIA Director said. Continuing, he added, "You all realise the importance of maintaining the status quo. What are your thoughts on the matter, Michael?"

"Only three other people outside this room currently know the truth. The President and his Chief of Staff and the Secretary of State and we would like to keep it that way for as long as possible. My agent Harry Steel doesn't even know the truth, even though his mission in Mozambique is to verify what we already believe is the truth," Michael Kurios Director of Counter Intelligence said. Continuing, he added, "I didn't like sending in one of my best agents into the field without the full brief, but I had no choice at this stage of the mission. We must maintain our silence until we're ready to release it to the world."

"Yes, well said, Michael. What are your thoughts, General Schneider?"

The general grimaced at the thought of what he knew but felt compelled to issue a warning to those gathered around the table. Leaning forward to make his presence felt, General Schneider Director of Operations said, "We're still not ready to match our enemy, right now, it could be at least another couple of years before I believe we'll be ready! In the meantime, I have the armed forces at a heightened level of readiness should we get attacked before then. None of the commanders of our air, sea and land forces knows the real reason why we're at this level of readiness; they all mistakenly believe it's pure practice. But, the longer we hide the truth the more likely someone lets the cat out of the bag."

"Thank you general for your thoughts. What about you Ruth?" Paul Henderson asked.

"My position hasn't changed since I heard the truth. It would've been better to inform the public; I believe it better than to try and maintain the secret. The general is right the longer this charade goes on the more likely someone spills the beans. Then the consequences are unknown as they were at the beginning of this mission. But, I understand the reasons for total secrecy," Ruth Gillingham Director of Internal Affairs replied.

"Yes, thanks for that Ruth, but the decision was made before your time. The reasons not to inform the public was made based on strategy and tactical warfare. We didn't want to alert our enemy and therefore give them an advantage in the expected coming war," Paul Henderson said. Continuing, he added, "What do you think, Anthony?"

"I think, it's essential that we maintain our secret until we're ready to match our enemy in battle. Otherwise, we give our enemy the advantage to strike at us before we're ready to respond in kind. It's our only viable option if we are to defeat our foe. Remember, they currently have a superior arsenal than we currently have. If General Schneider is right then we have to maintain our silence until we are fully prepared to act. And if that is another two years then so be it," Anthony Pagilia

Director of Espionage said.

"I take your point, Anthony. What are your thoughts, Julia?" Paul Henderson asked.

"We should maintain the status quo until we're ready to act. It would be foolhardy to act prematurely and thereby alerting our enemy to our intentions. I understand the reasons on both sides of the argument, but I maintain my view that it would be foolish to get caught with our pants down, so to speak," Julia Hayward Director of Special Operations replied.

Thank you, Julia, for your insight. What are your thoughts on the matter, George?" Paul Henderson asked.

"I think, the two schools of thought are both right on the matter. We're dammed if we don't and dammed if we do. But, I'm slightly in favour of the status quo. At the moment, the world continues to spin in its present state without the need for us to rock the boat. Our only chance is for us to gain the advantage is by maintaining our secret until we're ready to inform the public. I don't see another viable alternative," George Hammond Director of Communications replied.

"Yes, you're right George. So, pretty much everyone here goes with the status quo for the time being. I thank you all for your thoughts on the matter and I believe the right course of action is to maintain the secret until we're fully armed. As much as I would like to inform the public of our new enemy there comes a time when it's better to keep the public in the dark until we need to enlighten them. And as you know that will come soon enough," Paul Henderson Director of the CIA said regretfully. Continuing, he added, "Michael what's the latest in Mozambique?"

"As you know my agent Harry Steel is out there collaborating with a Russian agent who is also a biologist. He's only been there two days, so hasn't formulated any facts yet. We decided to collaborate with the Russians because they have a deep footprint in the country. It made access viable due to the Russian presence in the country, which they have been quietly developing the country's infrastructure and training their armed forces. Otherwise, we would have made it difficult for our agent to gather the facts. And as you know we need to know the facts before we can be certain of what to do. Even our agent doesn't know the real truth of his mission, which smacks of pointing the pony in the wrong direction. We should know more in a few more days," Michael Kurios Director of Counter Intelligence replied.

"Thank you, Michael. I'll convene another meeting when we know more," Paul Henderson Director of the CIA said before closing the meeting.

Chapter 5

On the island of Madagascar situated east of Mozambique's coastline, Dr. John Burrows was walking through the dense vegetation hoping to reach his jungle camp before nightfall. Some of the trees in the jungle were giants and reached taller than a six-storey building and most were over forty feet on average, so any light struggled to reach the jungle floor. As the doctor trekked through the jungle he could hear a constant buzzing noise emanating from the insects and crickets, which was interrupted by gibbons, birds and other animals making their presence known. Dr. John Burrows was a biologist studying the fauna and flora of the jungle for the United Nations (UN) and for other organisations, which supported his research financially in an ad hoc manner. Apart from a couple of local African men who he employed to help him around his jungle camp, he was as far away from society as one could get on the island of Madagascar.

John could hear his satellite phone ringing as he entered the large tent that served as his laboratory in the jungle. The canvas canopy that protected his belongings and lab equipment from the rain also kept out most of the mosquitoes that were a constant menace to him.

"Hello, is that Dr. John Burrows?" Harry asked.

"Yes, it's Dr. Burrows...who's talking?"

"Harry Steel of the CIA, I understand I can call on your help?" Harry asked. Harry knew the doctor was a local CIA asset and would be expected to help him when required.

"Yes, how can I help you?"

"Where are you now?" Harry asked.

"I'm in the middle of the jungle on the island of Madagascar," Dr. Burrows replied.

"Can you drop everything and get here to Mozambique."

"It will take me a few days, say around two days to get to Mozambique. I have a Cessna aeroplane waiting at a local airstrip. It's just the time it takes to get to the airfield. Once there it's only a short distance from there to Mozambique around two hours flight time to the coast of Mozambique. Where are you in Mozambique?" Dr. Burrows asked.

"I'm staying at Aerotel Hotel in Maputo the capital. Get here as soon as you can, I'll explain when you get here!" Harry said.

"Okay, copy that," Dr. Burrows said as the call ended. It was an inconvenience to drop everything when he had only just returned from Mozambique the day before. But, he knew his employers had their reasons and they partly funded his research into evolutionary biology.

On the trek, through the jungle, John had decided to make the journey with one of his workers as it was not safe to travel alone to the airfield. He wondered what kind of help the CIA wanted from him. His role as an asset was different from an agent; he was just an asset and not someone who conducted clandestine operations. His role was to work as normal and report any intelligence gathered to the CIA, and then occasionally have to work with other CIA operatives.

Dr. John Burrows was in his early thirties and had studied evolutionary biology from the University of Maryland and had been recruited into the CIA during his time at university. As a scientist, he jumped at the role of a CIA asset because of the extra funding he gained to help fund his research projects, which would otherwise be starved of funds. With his slender build, dark hair tied back into a ponytail and brown eyes, he cut an attractive figure for a female companion, but he had not found love since leaving university. His passion in life was his job and the esoteric theories he delved into in his spare time.

As John and his companion made a campfire for the night, he wondered why it was that man had made that great leap in knowledge over the last one hundred years compared to the last five thousand years, he said to himself. It was one way to help him get to sleep when all he could hear was the constant buzzing noise of millions of insects. He knew the fire would keep away most predators through the night, so he did not fear the night or the predators that lurked in the darkness. The last sound he could hear as he fell asleep that night was the noise of lemurs calling their mates high above in the forest canopy.

The following morning, they broke camp and continued their journey through the jungle to the airfield. At last, they could see the airfield and his Cessna parked on the perimeter of the airstrip. He told his companion to wait at the airfield for his return after they had made the aeroplane ready with fuel and supplies for the flight to Mozambique.

After take-off, he could relax for the next few hours while he crossed the stretch of ocean between the island and the Mozambique coastline. He had been told by Harry Steel to make his way to the village of Marupa where close by there was an airstrip where he could safely land. At the airfield, Harry was there with Olga to meet him. They had decided to wait for the doctor to arrive before finalising their questioning of Dr. Hamas at the Ebola outbreak in the nearby village.

"Hello, Dr. Burrows. My name is Harry Steel and this Dr Olga Domleic."

"We need your help in understanding the Ebola outbreak at the village," Olga said.

"Yes, that's fine."

"The CIA wants to know what's going on here…well that's the reason I've called you…for your expertise. I need to know what you think when we have finished interviewing Dr. Hamas at the village," Harry said.

"Hmm, I see…"

"Is that alright?"

"Yes, of course…let's get on our way then," Dr. Burrows said bluntly.

When they all had climbed into Harry's SUV, Harry then started to outline what they already knew about the other outbreaks they had visited and some of the doubts they had on the mission.

"Oh, by the way just call me John it saves time," Dr. Burrows said.

"I have my doubts and Olga has hers. Olga thinks there's a pattern to the outbreaks and I feel there's a fraud being conducted by persons unknown at present surrounding the WHO," Harry said.

"Yes, I see a pattern to the Ebola outbreaks when there shouldn't be one!" Olga stressed.

"I will know more when I've seen it for myself," Dr. Burrows said.

"I'll show you later what I mean," Olga said strenuously.

"I see a massive fraud, but I don't have any proof just yet, it's only a theory so far," Harry remarked.

"Based on what?" Dr. Burrows asked as Harry negotiated his vehicle through the numerous potholes along the dirt track that led to the village. At least, it was not raining, otherwise, the track would be a complete mud bath and unpassable, he surmised.

"Based on the fact that money corrupts and Africa is rife with corruption and it wouldn't take much to corrupt some of the locals. In my experience, the two things that make people do what they don't usually do are money and sex. I don't think sex is the one, so it's money! And the thorny issue of why my employers decided to send me here? I'm not here to hold Olga's hand even as pretty as she is," Harry said, smiling.

"Is that it?" Dr. Burrows said incredulously.

"No, there's more, I'll tell you later when we're finished interviewing Dr. Hamas."

"Okay, and you…Olga what's your story?" Dr. Burrows asked bluntly.

"Similar story, I was asked by my employers the Russian government to assist the CIA in understanding what's going on here with the Ebola outbreaks. They obviously felt Harry needed help!" Olga said smiling.

"Isn't unusual for Russia and America to be collaborating on a mission such as this?" Dr. Burrows asked curiously.

"Yes, but we do collaborate in areas such as the space program and other areas that are just not talked about. Even though we're meant to be enemies it's surprising how much we do work together it's just not fashionable to be open about it. Both countries see the need to stop world wars from happening. In the Second World War, we lost over thirty million people, which delayed the progress of the country. For many years after the war, Russia struggled to feed its citizens because of the lack of investment in the farming industry. We didn't have the modern tractors or the people willing to work the land in an efficient manner," Olga said.

"Oh, right…I see…"

"Yes, okay…"

"I've never worked in this part of Mozambique before," Dr. Burrows remarked. Continuing, he added, "How long before we get there?"

"Not long now, about twenty minutes," Harry replied as he tried to avoid the many potholes along the dirt track.

"Olga, you said there's a pattern to the Ebola outbreaks and there shouldn't be, is that right?" Dr. Burrows asked. Continuing, he added, "Can you explain your reasoning?"

"Having seen three outbreaks and done a search on the Internet of all the Ebola outbreaks throughout Mozambique you will see a pattern. When there shouldn't be one. I'm a biologist and not an epidemiologist, but from my experience in biology, there shouldn't be a pattern because that's not how a virus works. We know the Ebola virus is highly contagious and spreads from person to person and doesn't confine itself to a particular area. It moves out and spreads like a flood of water. We were told they stopped the spread of the virus by stopping all contact within each village to the outside world. But, if you research other Ebola outbreaks across the African continent you will see that those outbreaks continued into the towns and cities and not like the outbreaks we have in Mozambique," Olga said.

"I see what you are saying, and you could be right. So, what is your synopsis of the outbreaks?" Dr. Burrows asked.

"Well, to put it bluntly, the outbreaks are artificial!" Olga said pensively.

"That could be the reason why I feel there's a massive fraud taking place," Harry interjected.

Suddenly, Harry stopped the car as he noticed two armed Africans dressed in combat uniforms up ahead waiting to stop their vehicle. Immediately, they could hear the background noise of the jungle buzzing.

"Get your gun out, Olga," Harry demanded as he

reached for his Glock-19 gun strapped inside his shoulder holster. As he watched the two men approach the car he was ready with his gun to react to whatever happened.

Suddenly, the two guerrillas raised their AK47's ready to open fire when Olga and Harry opened fire and killing both with several shots at their bodies. Their training had kicked in and every gunshot hit their target. Harry and Olga made a thorough search of the two guerrillas and from their identity cards found they came from the neighbouring country of Zimbabwe. Then Harry and Olga quickly dragged the two guerrillas into the cover of the bush and took their machine guns and ammunition for possible later use. Harry and Olga knew about the guerrilla war that was currently taking place in some parts of Mozambique, but they both had not realised its tentacles had reached this far south.

"They must be Al Shabaab fighters," Harry remarked.

"Yes, I agree," Olga agreed.

"Let's cover the bodies, and hope they're never found," Harry suggested as he began to cover the bodies with vegetation from the bush. When he and Olga were satisfied the bodies were well hidden from the dirt track they got back into their vehicle and continued their journey.

"Shit! That was a close call, I thought for a moment we were all dead," Dr. Burrows remarked. He had joined the CIA as an asset and not as an agent and was not expecting to see any action, he said to himself.

"Yes, well that's why Olga and I are here, if it had been three doctors travelling along this road, today, then it's probable they'd be all dead. Those guerrillas wanted our vehicle and whatever else they could steal from us. And then they would've killed us all. They were

Al Shabaab fighters. It's a terrorist group that sows destruction wherever they go. They kill and murder those they come across in their desire to install their doctrine on a country. They're affiliated to Al-Qaeda the Islamist organisation, which wants to overthrow Muslim and non-Muslim countries and impose their rule," Harry said.

"Yes, I've heard of them."

"I didn't think they would operate this far south," Olga remarked.

"Perhaps, they see easy pickings!" Dr. Burrows said.

"Well, those two fighters probably had it coming in the scheme of things. Their time was up. Fate had decided their time was up," Harry said.

"What do you mean?" Dr. Burrows asked.

"They didn't expect us to fire back as they went for their weapons. We were trained to act faster, which they hadn't counted on. They were dead before they hit the ground. Fate played a hand and our shots were accurate and every bullet hit its target!" Harry said nonchalantly.

"What do you mean fate?" Dr. Burrows asked curiously.

"Fate has a way of finding its direction. Just suppose for a minute, that those two fighters were better trained, and then equally they would have had the same amount of time to fire their weapons at us. But, they were also greedy; they didn't want to wreck the car because they saw it as a cash cow. Their hesitation cost them their lives, now, who knows what crimes they've committed while members of Al Shabaab. For all we know they're angels but I doubt it. In war, no one knows who gets killed or not. Their time was up and they met us. Olga knows it's about microseconds that save lives," Harry

said.

Olga just winced at the suggestion of pity for the two terrorists; she knew what was probably on the cards if she survived. Harry was right, those fighters call it what you like were up to no good. Olga noticed straight away they weren't regular Mozambique soldiers' by-the-way they were dressed as did Harry no doubt, Olga thought.

"What do you think Olga?" Harry asked briskly.

"I don't have any doubts," Olga said. She knew what was on the cards if she survived. The terrorists would have probably raped her and killed her later, she thought. She did not have any mercy in her body for the terrorists and would kill again if she had to, she said to herself.

***

As they drove into the village they immediately saw the death and destruction, and they could hear dogs howling for their owners and birds squawking in the trees. The dead were strewn all around the village with bodies riddled with bullets. Blood was everywhere. People lay where they tried to escape the carnage, outside their homes, and in the village square. Some of the causalities were children killed next to their mothers holding their babies.

When Harry knelt down and felt the temperature of a still-warm body he realised the attack on the village had taken place only perhaps an hour earlier. He also noticed the body of the doctor he had spoken to the day before. The carnage had all the hallmarks of an Al Shabaab attack and he wondered how close the terrorists were to the village. Not far, he said to himself.

"What sickens me is the total waste of life these Al Shabaab terrorists creates in their endeavour to stamp their message across the country. They're totally out of control. The sooner Mozambique deals with the problem by killing every one of the bastards the better the country will be. I don't have any time or mercy for the bastards. I'm ready to kill again to avenge the innocent," Harry said philosophically.

Dr. Burrows looked inside the hospital tent and saw all the patients had been shot in their beds. No one was spared. Blood was everywhere he looked. Harry grimaced at the sight of the carnage inside the tent. Blood was splattered all over the inside of the tent and on the floor and Harry imagined the scene as the terrorists would have fired their machineguns around the tent. Olga winced at the sight inside the tent and wondered if the terrorists knew what they were doing when they killed the Ebola patients. There would have been blood flying everywhere and the potential for infection to spread to the killers, she said herself.

"We better get the hell out of here," Olga said sharply. She knew the potential for catching the virus was high in such a scenario.

"Yeah, the sooner the better," Dr. Burrows agreed. He also could see the danger and he had not signed up for such dangerous situations with the CIA. He felt sick with what he had witnessed and was white as a ghost.

"Yes, before they come back, otherwise, we could become their next victims," Harry said regretfully. Harry was not worried but just concerned for the doctor and Olga. Harry had reconciled the thought of catching a bullet many times and had come to the conclusion that when his time was up then it was no point in worrying because worrying never stopped a bullet.

They quickly started their journey back to the capital through the jungle and back onto the highway. Shortly, after getting onto the highway Harry noticed the lack of traffic coming in the opposite direction and wondered why. Farther along the road he saw through his binoculars a group of men blocking the highway. He saw they were terrorists and immediately stopped his vehicle.

"Look! There are terrorists blocking the highway up ahead," Harry shouted and passed the binoculars to Olga. Through the binoculars, Olga could see the ragtag of men waving their weapons and immediately could see they were up to no good.

"Shit! What are we going to do?" Dr. Burrows asked. He was already shaking all over his body from the previous events that day and wondered where it would all end. He did not want this kind of action in his life, he was a scientist and not a soldier, he said to himself.

"We will go back and get to your aeroplane from a different road, it's our only option. Are you alright John you're shaking?" Harry asked calmly. John just nodded his head with affirmation.

Harry pulled the car over and with Olga studied a map and looked for another route to the airfield. Harry and Olga could only see one option, but it made a considerable detour to get to the airfield. They would have to go back into the bush for several miles and then make their way around the roadblock to get to the airfield.

"This looks like the only route around that roadblock. If we follow this dirt track through that village then we should avoid those men. Then it's only a few miles to the airfield. Let's try that!" Harry stated.

A short distance along the highway they turned onto a dirt track and back into the jungle. A few miles into their journey they came across the village, which had also been the scene of a massacre. Al Shabaab had been busy killing everyone and leaving no one alive.

Harry continued onwards not wishing to stop for survivors because he knew the chance of finding any survivors was next to zero. Suddenly, a young African boy came running out from behind a house and Harry immediately stopped the SUV. The boy was crying.

"What happened here?" Harry asked.

"Al Shabaab killed everyone and I hid under my house and saw what they did," the boy said, crying.

"Okay, get in," Harry demanded.

"How many men with guns did you see?" Harry asked the boy.

"I counted about twelve, but maybe more. They took some of the girls and women away with them," the boy replied.

"Stop crying! What's your name and how old are you?" Olga asked.

"I'm nine years old and my name is Ishmael," the boy said.

"We'll get you to safety," Harry said. Continuing, he added, "John, will you give the boy some water and any food we have."

"Eh, yeah…"

"It looks like Al Shabaab are having a major assault on the surrounding villages and we have to be careful not to run into them. I've only one spare clip of ammunition and what's in my Glock. What about you, Olga?" Harry asked.

"About the same, but we do have the machine guns with three clips of ammunition," Olga replied.

Suddenly, Harry stopped the car on top of the brow of a hill and reached for his binoculars and saw in the distance a group of fighters walking along the river bank with a group of women. Then suddenly, gunfire rattled Harry's car as if like a series of firecrackers going off.

"Take cover!" Olga shouted.

"Get down! Get out on the left side and hide behind that hill, while I'll drive the car back behind the hill," Harry said hurriedly while pointing to the hill beside the car. Harry was immediately concerned for his passengers and not himself.

"What are we going to do?" Dr. Burrows asked in a panic. His tone of voice revealed the fear he felt.

"Get behind that boulder there and I'll go down to the river and outflank them. Shoot anything that comes close, but conserve our ammunition," Harry demanded.

Harry quickly circled the terrorist's position and saw what he had to do. He had to be precise as he only had enough bullets for each of the men. He soon found a sniper's position for cover, but with an excellent view of the terrorists' position. He took aim and made every bullet count. As soon as the terrorists knew what was happening they quickly panicked and started to run in all directions. Harry made sure that no one escaped his justice. Within minutes, there was just one fighter alive, but slowly bleeding to death.

"Why are you attacking the villages in this area?" Harry asked as he pushed his boot into the man's wound and made him scream in pain.

"Because we're short of funds and food," the fighter said.

"Is that necessary?" Dr. Burrows asked.

"No, but he's dying anyway, don't have pity for a murderer John," Harry said forcibly.

"How many fighters are there in this area?"

Harry pushed his boot again into the man's wound and again the fighter screamed in pain. He continued until the man was willing to give up the information. The fighter grimaced and winced at Harry's action, but soon relented.

"The main force is about fifty strong and is heading towards the airfield they hope to find supplies. They have three armoured trucks," the fighter said.

"What are we going to do with him?" Dr. Burrows asked.

"Nothing, he's already dying in twenty minutes his organs will fail."

The fighter looked up at Harry for pity as Olga shot the man in the head and put him out of his misery. That was the only choice they had there were no medical facilities nearby if they wanted to save the terrorist, he would be dead before they arrived at the nearest hospital.

Harry and Olga then untied the captured women and sent them back to their village with the young boy Ismael and then they continued on their journey to the airfield. As they got close to the airfield they could see smoke rising above the buildings in the distance, which was not a good omen. They decided to park far from the airfield and to take a look from a distance at what was happening at the airfield. Dr. Burrows was the first to see his aeroplane in flames amongst all the other destruction the terrorists had committed.

"It's no use, we're too late to save the plane," Dr. Burrows said.

"Yes, there's no point waiting around, let's get the hell out of here," Harry said.

"Yeah, back to civilisation," Olga said.

They travelled along bush dirt tracks that ran almost parallel to the main highway until they considered it was safe to return to the highway. Once, on the highway, they immediately saw traffic in both directions and noticed Mozambique army vehicles heading in the opposite direction.

"Well, John you'll have to stay in Maputo until

you can acquire another aeroplane. Besides, we need you here for a while, until we sort out what's going on here. We'll find another outbreak to visit and you can give us your synopsis. In the meantime, it's best if you stay at the same hotel as us…the Aerotel Hotel we're staying there," Harry said.

"Yes, that's fine. Do you plan to inform the authorities about what we have seen?" Dr. Burrows asked.

"No, it would only complicate our stay here," Harry said.

"Yes, I agree," Olga agreed.

After driving for another hour they finally made it to the outskirts of the capital and saw another group of army vehicles heading north out of the city. As they parked at the hotel they saw the damage to the car, which had a series of bullet holes that peppered the vehicle as if a colander. Harry was not worried the CIA would take care of the cost; he was more concerned about wrapping up the case and getting back to America as soon as possible. The thought of many more days being attacked by mosquitos and his throat choking for air in the heat bothered him.

"We'll meet in the hotel bar in say about an hour," Harry said to Olga and John. "I need to freshen up."

"Yes, me too…" Olga said.

***

Later, Harry was already in the hotel bar enjoying a JD and coke when Olga arrived with John. Harry had already been on the Internet and found another Ebola outbreak to visit, which was only an hour's drive from the capital.

"Look!" Harry pointed to the village on the map. "This outbreak is due west of the city and not far.

Hopefully, we can avoid any Al Shabaab in that area. But, just in case, I've reloaded my Glock and have spare ammunition. What about you, Olga?"

"Yes, I've done the same and we still have all the weapons in the car we collected from those dead Al Shabaab fighters," Olga replied.

"Not all, I gave some to those women for protection," Harry remarked.

"What about me?" Dr. Burrows asked.

"Here take this, it's fully loaded," Harry said as he handed the doctor another handgun. "If you run out then grab one of those AK47 to use." Continuing, he added, "In the meantime, order a drink quickly and let's get going."

"We better use my vehicle, it's least likely to fail," Olga said, smiling.

"Okay, good idea, we'll transfer the AK47"s to your vehicle," Harry said as they transferred the weapons to Olga's car, before making their way to the outskirts of the city, and onto a dirt track that led deep into the bush and jungle. As they travelled along the track they saw in the distance the peaks of the mountains that appeared covered in vegetation like a green carpet. Occasionally, they stopped to check their bearings and all they could hear was the incessant buzzing of the jungle and the occasional lemur call.

During the journey, Harry outlined his plan for the day. He wanted John to steer the interview while Harry and Olga would just observe the proceedings. Harry felt that it would be useful to take a back seat and analyse the information gleaned. Olga had agreed to Harry's plan. She also felt it would be useful to take a back seat while John conducted the questioning.

Olga carefully steered the car away from giant potholes along the dirt track and finally saw the village and parked outside the village. They saw the white tent and many people wandering about as they walked towards the field hospital.

"Who's in charge?" Dr. Burrows asked politely. A young African boy pointed to the tent.

"Who's in charge?" Dr. Burrows asked again with an authoritative tone of voice.

"I am."

"My name is Dr Burrows and you?"

"My name is Dr Almelo Sanchez."

"I'm here from the WHO and would like to ask you some questions."

"Yes, go ahead."

"When did the Ebola outbreak start here?" Dr. Burrows asked as Harry and Olga just looked on.

"It didn't, well, we first thought it was an Ebola outbreak, but it turned out to be Dengue Fever, not Ebola. But, just as deadly," Dr. Sanchez said.

"Oh, I see, what drugs are you using to combat the fever?" Dr. Burrows asked.

"Remdesivir and Dexamethasone both are working well," Dr. Sanchez said.

"But aren't those drugs used for Ebola patients?" Dr. Burrows asked incredulously.

"Yes, but they are also used for Dengue Fever. They are not a cure but help boost an immune response, which seems to work," Dr. Sanchez said.

"What is the mortality rate," Dr. Burrows asked.

"Around twenty-five per cent, before we had these drugs the mortality rate was nearer seventy-five per cent," Dr. Sanchez said.

"Is there anything unusual about the outbreak?" Dr. Burrows asked.

"Yes, we haven't seen an outbreak of Dengue Fever in this part of the world before this one," Dr.

Sanchez said.

"Have you any thoughts on why this is the case?" Dr. Burrows asked.

"Not particularly, it's just unusual…normally Dengue fever is found nearer the Arabian countries and not down here. The mosquitoes that transmit the disease are found up there, so it's a mystery why we have it down here. It's not a disease that transmits from person to person you can only catch it from a female mosquito bite. The Dengue virus lives inside the mosquito," Dr. Sanchez said.

"Why is the Internet still showing this outbreak as Ebola?" Dr. Burrows asked abruptly.

Shrugging his shoulders, Dr. Sanchez replied, "Like I said before we initially thought the outbreak was Ebola and the person or persons who wrote that information on the Internet haven't bothered to update the Internet."

Have you adequate funding from the WHO to fight this outbreak?" Dr. Burrows asked.

"Yes, we've had no problems with funds. In fact, I was surprised how easy it was to obtain funding for this outbreak from the WHO, normally, they're last in line to put their hands in their pockets if you know what I mean," Dr. Sanchez replied.

"Have you noticed any patterns appearing in the Ebola outbreaks in this country?" Dr. Burrows asked.

"No, can't say I have, but then again I've been busy saving people's lives to notice any patterns," Dr. Sanchez replied. Continuing, he added, "Is there a pattern?"

"Well, there may be one. Doesn't an outbreak spread out like floodwater, normally?" Dr. Burrows replied. Continuing, he added, "The Ebola outbreaks in Mozambique have been isolated incidents, which is contrary to the norm."

"Yes, I see what you're saying. Now, that you point this out I can see why you think it's not normal. What does WHO think?" Dr. Sanchez asked intently.

"We don't know, that's why we're here to find out and report back to them," Dr. Burrows replied.

"Oh, I see."

"Ouch!"

"Dam mosquitos one of them has just bitten me."

"Are there any other issues you found odd or suspicious?" Dr. Burrows asked.

"Yes, when I was first asked to come here, I'd spent time at other outbreaks and we noticed that different strains of the virus were at work. Normally, from my previous experience with Ebola, you get infections with the same strain of the virus. Especially, within the same country, the virus doesn't normally mutate that fast. You may see different strains of the virus appear in different countries, but not in the same country as it has appeared in Mozambique," Dr. Sanchez replied.

"Have you any ideas or reasons for this anomaly?" Dr. Burrows asked.

"Shit! Another mosquito has just bitten me on the ankle…"

"The little bastards…"

"Did you hear that?"

"Yeah, that was just a lemur calling its mate, most likely."

"What…yes…"

"No, can't say I have, I've been too busy saving lives to think on it too deeply. But, it has been rattling around in my mind for some time and I believe with other doctors dealing with the Ebola outbreaks in this country. From conversations, I've had via email with other doctors in the field it would seem to be a common anomaly. But, I remember one doctor voiced her concerns early on with the WHO and was told that they would look into it, but as far as I know no one has heard a word or anything about the subject back from the WHO," Dr. Sanchez replied.

"Do you remember the doctor's name who voiced their concerns?" Dr. Burrows asked.

"Yes, let me think…yes the doctor was Dr. Sheila Atwell. She was one of the first doctors to discover the Ebola virus in Mozambique. I believe, she's working on the mosquito problem in this country. I think, she's based in Maputo, but I'm not sure. All I know is when she raised her concerns about the Ebola anomaly she was suddenly transferred away from the Ebola project, which wasn't expected. I understand from colleagues that she was quite upset about leaving her Ebola patients at the time. I have her phone number if you'd like to speak to her," Dr. Sanchez replied.

"Yes, that would be helpful. Now, is there anything else you think we should know before we leave you to your patients?" Dr. Burrows asked. Continuing, he added, "Oh, nearly forgot, have there been any signs of Al Shabaab in the area?"

"No, that's it and there has been no sign of Al Shabaab in the area. The Mozambique army are well entrenched in the surrounding area, so I doubt whether we will see those terrorists in this area," Dr. Sanchez replied.

"Well, take care, you know about the recent attacks by Al Shabaab up north?" Dr. Burrows asked.

"Yes, it's been all over the radio news broadcasts this afternoon," Dr. Sanchez replied.

"Okay, thanks for your help, we'll be on our way…thanks again for your help," Dr. Burrows said as

Harry and Olga also thanked the doctor.

As they got into their vehicle Harry was already phoning Dr. Sheila Atwell before they drove back to the city.

"Hello, is that Dr. Atwell?"

"Yes, speaking...who's asking?"

"Hi, my name is Harry Steel would it be possible to meet today. I understand you're in Maputo is that correct?" Harry asked.

"Yes, I'm currently working from a building situated along the main river, near the glass factory on Mt. Pleasant Street, you can't miss it...its painted green and the only building with that colour. Number forty-two. In say an hour from now, is that okay?" Dr. Sheila Atwell replied.

"Yes, we may be a little later, is that okay?"

"Yes, that's fine...can I ask what you want from me?" Dr. Atwell asked.

"We just want to ask you a few questions about the Ebola outbreaks in Mozambique; we got your number from Dr. Sanchez. Is that okay?" Harry asked.

"Yes, that's fine...see you later," Dr. Atwell said before hanging up the call.

"Put your foot down, Olga, I want to make the city before it gets dark. We don't want to get stuck out here in the jungle when it gets dark tout suite," Harry remarked. Harry and Olga were intrigued by what Dr. Sanchez had said about Dr. Atwell concerning the Ebola outbreaks and felt they were on to something. Dr. Burrows also had the same feelings about Dr. Atwell and was also eager to see what she had to say on the matter.

***

After an hour of travelling back along the dirt track, they soon came across the main highway leading back to Maputo. On the outskirts of the city, they used their Satnav to find the address they were looking for. It was only a short distance across the city when the Satnav announced the address they were looking for. It wasn't hard to miss as Dr. Atwell had described a green building that stuck out like a sore thumb in the surrounding area. As Harry, Olga and Dr. Burrows entered the building they were greeted by Dr. Sheila Atwell who was in her mid-thirties with long blond hair down to her shoulders and blue eyes.

"Hi, my name is Harry Steel and this is Dr Olga Domleic and Dr John Burrows...we spoke on the phone."

"Yes, my name is Dr Sheila Atwell, how can I help?"

"We understand you were removed from your work with an Ebola outbreak when you started to raise concerns? Harry asked.

"Yes, that's correct, who told you?" Dr. Atwell asked.

"Dr. Almelo Sanchez mentioned it."

"What were your concerns about the Ebola outbreak?" Dr. Burrows asked.

"Yes, I was one of the first doctors to recognise the Ebola virus in a small village just south of the capital. My initial concerns about the virus to the WHO were not well received because within a day I was transferred here. I was initially upset about leaving my patients, but now I'm happy to be doing this work with mosquitoes. I raised my concerns about how the Ebola outbreak had started because normally the virus spreads like a wildfire without limits on its infection spread. We saw outbreaks occurring all over Mozambique, yet we saw no outbreaks in nearby countries, which is not the norm. And the outbreaks were confined to small out of the way villages and not in any densely populated areas, such as towns and cities. I just felt it was odd and needed further investigation by the WHO. I was just doing my job and raising my concerns," Dr. Atwell said.

"You saw a pattern, is that correct?" Olga asked with a worried tone of voice.

"Yes, how did you know?" Dr. Atwell asked.

"I saw the same pattern when there shouldn't be one," Olga stressed.

"Was that your only concern?" Dr. Burrows asked intently.

"No, I had been in contact with other doctors via email who were dealing with other Ebola outbreaks and we noticed by examining the DNA of the virus that each virus was a different strain. Now, this isn't normal. You normally find the virus will mutate over time, but these viruses were totally different strains like from the same family but different parents. This to me was a big red alert. So, I raised my concerns with Dr. Fellows at the WHO, only to find the next day I had been transferred here. And since then, I've heard not a word about my concerns from the WHO," Dr. Atwell said.

"What's your synopsis of the Ebola outbreaks?" Harry asked briskly. He was intrigued to find out as much as possible from the doctor. He wanted to wrap the case up and get back to the States as soon as possible.

"It's almost as if the outbreaks have been planted by someone and there is an experiment going on, it's the only logical conclusion. I don't have any solid proof just circumstantial evidence and my gut feeling. But, I trust my instinct with my life," Dr. Atwell replied.

"Snap! I feel the same," Olga said.

"So, you haven't continued with your research into the Ebola outbreaks?" Dr. Burrows asked.

"No, been too busy here understanding why we have a Dengue Fever outbreak in Mozambique. The female Aedes mosquito hosts the virus, but it normally lives in the northern part of Africa around the Arabian countries and not this far south. Again, this is not normal behaviour. But, it could be down to climate change and other environmental changes. I'm not sure at present," Dr. Atwell replied.

"Could the two be related?" Harry asked.

"What do you mean?"

"You said you had a feeling that someone planted the Ebola virus here could that be the case with the Dengue Fever?" Harry replied.

"I see what you mean, you could be right, but I hadn't linked the two," Dr. Atwell said.

"Perhaps, they're linked and not just a coincidence," Harry suggested, smiling.

Harry saw the frustration on the doctor's face with his last comment and wondered if he had struck a chord. He also noticed the look on Olga's and John's faces as if they did not believe in coincidences and he was right on the money. Harry felt at that moment he was right and the thought of a coincidence did not fit the bill, he said to himself.

"If the two are linked then do you think the WHO is involved somehow?" Dr. Burrows asked.

"Yeah, but I've no proof, but that Dr. Fellows at the WHO is involved, I'd put money on him if I was a gambling person and I'm not. I found him condescending and unreliable," Dr. Atwell replied.

When the doctor had shown Harry, Olga and Dr. Burrows her laboratory where large glass sealed spaces were being used to breed and house different species of mosquito. They thanked the doctor for her time and help and they then returned to their vehicle. Outside it was dark. The only light available was from the full moon and Harry noticed a car parked up the street with two occupants inside and wondered if they were being followed. He was immediately concerned for Dr. Atwell's safety and returned to see the doctor to her car and watched as she safely drove away. Harry watched the car up the street follow their car as they headed back to their hotel. He expressed his concern to Olga and John and told them to stop at the next street corner and told them to wait in the car as he went around the block of buildings to come up behind the spurious vehicle. Harry needed to know who was following their car and who they worked for. He had his Glock in his hand and was ready to use it when he confronted the two individuals.

"Don't make a move or I'll shoot!" Continuing, he added, "Who are you and who do you work for?"

"We were hired by the WHO to follow you," the man said.

"Who hired you?"

"Dr. Fellows."

"What do you want to know?" Harry asked as he hit one of the men nearest to him across the face with his gun.

"Where you go and who you see," the man said in shock from the hit on his face.

"Show me your ID"s, if I see you again I will kill you both, is that understood? And don't bother visiting Dr. Atwell, otherwise, I will find you both and kill you. Is that understood?" Harry stressed.

Suddenly, one of the men reached for his gun and Harry pushed the other man into the other as the man fired his gun at Harry just missing him by inches. Harry then fired off two bullets killing both men instantly, and then he quietly walked back to the car and looking to see if anyone had witnessed the event. He told Olga and John what had happened and told them to help him put the dead men into the boot of their car and to drive into the bush.

"Was that really necessary?" Dr. Burrows asked pensively.

"They fired first!" Harry replied sharply. In his mind, Harry knew he had no choice but to react and ask questions later. Besides, the CIA had carte blanche to carry out their missions with deadly force if it needed to such was the power and influence they had around the world, he said to himself.

On the way, Harry stopped and bought a container of petrol. In the bush, Harry and John tossed the bodies into the thick vegetation and set light to the two dead men and waited until the fire had consumed the bodies and any evidence.

Chapter 6

Later, back at the hotel, Harry, Olga and Dr. Burrows gathered in the hotel bar and began to exchange notes on how they felt about the mission.

With a JD in one hand, Harry said, "I've more questions than answers at the moment. What's your view, John?"

"We need to interview Dr. Fellows at the WHO and see what he has to say," John replied. Continuing, he added, "But, now I know more since speaking to Dr. Atwell there's more to this mystery than meets the eye."

"What about you, Olga, what's your view?"

"First, I need to order another vodka that smoke from the burning bodies got right to the back of my throat, thanks to Harry's actions," Olga said.

"Well, I had no choice it was them or me. I'm not here to get married; I'm not holding anyone's hand. I've got a mission to complete and sometimes you have to kill people," Harry said.

"Yes, I agree," Olga agreed, smiling.

"One hell of a fraud, I believe is going on. I don't have proof just circumstantial evidence. The evidence from Dr. Atwell should be enough to set the alarm bells ringing. When something is acting unnaturally we then expect human hands involved for whatever purpose. Sometimes it's just money or sex that drives people to be easily corrupted. I confront the devil on most days so I'm very much a cynic," Harry said.

"I said, from the beginning, that there was a pattern when there shouldn't be one. That's another piece of circumstantial evidence to add to Harry's list," Olga said, smiling.

"And the appearance of Dengue Fever is another piece of circumstantial evidence to add to the list. All in all, a cesspit of evidence that means something big is occurring," John said confidently.

"But what government or individual would gain from such actions?" Olga asked sceptically.

"That's why we're here. To find the culprits," Harry said.

"Yes, find the bastards!" Olga said with a commanding tone of voice.

"Yes, tomorrow we will know more," Dr. Burrows said matter-of-factly.

Then Dr. Burrows told them about his research in Madagascar. While Harry and Olga listened to John explain his reasons why as a biologist, he had a different opinion from the established view considering anthropology and evolution. He first explained that a biologist studies animals, plants and organisms in their natural environment by understanding their genetics and what affects them such as pollution.

"Have you heard about "the special event theory" that theorises a special event must have taken place around forty thousand to fifty thousand years ago? This is when we started to paint figures and animals on cave walls. This is also the time when we started to make sophisticated tools. Before that, we had used the same flint stone tools for at least a million years. And then they assume language came at around the same time. Now, the Homo erectus our ancestors evolved around two hundred thousand years ago into what we call a modern man or Homo sapiens. It was a long time and consistent with the Darwinian view of evolution and the theory of "natural selection" espoused by Darwin. Don't you think that it is strange our progress suddenly speeded up going against the Darwinian view of evolution? Even Darwin had his doubts about his theory because he could not reconcile how our intelligence had suddenly evolved so quickly…this went against his theory of "natural selection" that he almost didn't publish his theory," John explained.

"That's a long time to be using the same tools without progress. So, why is that?" Harry asked.

"Yes, it is…that's why it's such a mystery! I'm not sure what the truth is because there're so many missing links in our evolution that it is difficult to come down on one side or the other, but I do favour "the special event theory" because it makes sense to me," Dr. Burrows replied.

"How does that differ from the established view?" Olga asked. Even though she was a biologist she had not heard of "the special event theory" before and was intrigued to hear what the doctor had to say on the matter.

"Normally, it takes millions of years for evolution to adapt and change to its environment by a means of "natural selection" that is the Darwinian view of our evolution and not this "special event theory" that some scientists and anthropologists postulate. It is the time that's the difference between the two. The gap between the two is as wide as the Grand Canyon and I don't see it narrowing any time soon," John said.

"So, is that your view doctor?" Harry asked.

"I'm still on the fence, but it makes a lot of sense for many smart people. And it would answer an anomaly that exists in how women give birth. Women nearly die from giving birth and you have to ask the question why that is the case. Don't you think evolution would've solved that problem over the aeons of time? Other animals don't have the same problem giving birth as we do as a species," John replied.

"I take your point, doctor…that's an anomaly for sure. Never looked too deeply into the issue before, but, you're right it's a major flaw in Darwin's theory of evolution for our species," Harry said. Even though Harry was not a biologist or anthropologist he could see the merit in what Dr. Burrows was explaining. There were anomalies in much of our evolution that did not make sense to any sensible person, he said to himself.

"Does that mean we have to class you as a radical doctor?" Olga asked, laughing. She knew the doctor was on to something and she would investigate further when she got back to Russia even though she had taken much of what the doctor had said in a light-hearted way.

"Yes, I guess so or someone who thinks outside of the box," John replied. Continuing, he added, "Consider history which is often being rewritten as we find out more about our past. We now know Christopher Columbus wasn't the first person to find the American continent it was the Vikings. And it was around five hundred years before we were sure about that part of history." Dr. Burrows said.

Dr. John Burrows continued to explain his views to Harry and Olga. He explained that biology was the study of humans, plants and animals, and the environments in which they exist. He went on to explain that currently, his research was the study of fruit bats and how they exist in an ecosystem. He explained what benefits the fruit bats provide to their ecosystem and how other plants and animals interact with their presence. Dr. Burrows explained that his research was still in its early stages and because of lack of funds progress had been slow. He told Harry and Olga that governments were short-sighted and he believed that the study of fruit bats would reveal new insights into vaccine research. Dr. Burrows explained that fruit bats have thousands of viruses in their bodies and the Covid-19 virus, which caused the recent pandemic. The fact that the fruit bat is unaffected by being a carrier of the Covid-19 virus should send alarm bells ringing. The scientific community are pretty confident the Covid-19 virus came from the fruit bats, but the jury is still out on how it was transmitted to humans. The Chinese were not keen to have an early inquiry, so it's plausible that it was not an act of God, but a human hand had played a part the doctor explained. Dr. Burrows explained that perhaps, someone in a laboratory somewhere got careless and they inadvertently spread its destruction on society by accident.

"What have you learned so far, or is it too early?" Harry asked as if genuinely interested in what the doctor was studying. He was getting tired of the lecture and seeking to get to bed.

"Well, fruit bats have been around for millions of years and have naturally evolved to deal with pathogens such as a virus. And equally, humans have evolved at the same time, now don't you think the chance of cross-infection would be nearer zero? We as a species, so we're told spent millions of year's cohabitating in the jungles and the forests with the fruit bats, and most likely we caught and ate them. We would have built up immunity over the aeons of time, just like the fruit bats have. They said the Ebola outbreaks were initially caused by fruit bats. It just doesn't stack up in my view." Continuing, he added, "Now, do you see how important my research is?"

"Yes, I see what you're saying, John. My work as a biologist has taken me all around the world. Normally, I'm tasked to aid a country with its crisis. I saw a pattern here when there shouldn't be one. Tomorrow, we'll see what Dr. Fellows has to say for himself. I didn't trust the man, the moment, I saw him look me up and down as if I was his blow-up doll," Olga said, smiling. She was a good judge of character by the body language of a person, and Dr. Fellows she categorised as seedy, she said to herself.

"Seedy and probably greedy, I have no doubt about that being a motive for our Dr. Fellows," Harry said. He felt sure that Dr. Fellows was deep into something bad and was willing to call out the doctor, tomorrow. Harry could not wait to solve the case and return to the States as soon as possible.

"See you in the morning, I'm off to bed," Dr. Burrows said.

"Me too, I need the rest and my beauty sleep," Harry agreed, smiling.

"Copy that," Olga said.

***

It was a hot and sticky morning as Harry, Olga and Dr. Burrows made their way to the WHO headquarters in the southern part of Maputo for their meeting with Dr. Fellows. The traffic was particularly busy that day as they pulled up outside the building and parked.

***

"I'm glad you could spare the time again to see us," Harry said.

"How can I help?" Dr. Fellows asked.

"My name is Dr. John Burrows, I would like to know what progress have you made on the concerns that Dr. Atwell outlined to you before she was transferred to her present position at the mosquito laboratory here in Maputo," Dr. Burrows asked.

"Ummm, I don't recall that conversation. Perhaps, our security team handled it, I'm not sure, will have to get back to you at a later date," Dr. Fellows said anxiously. He had not forgotten, he just did not have an answer to give.

"Well, to cut to the chase, we think a massive fraud is taking place and you're in the middle of it," Olga said aggressively. She was not worried about how the doctor felt about being labelled a thief.

"What evidence do you have?" Dr. Fellows said snappily.

"Enough to sink you to the bottom of the cesspit," Harry said nonchalantly.

"You may be just the tip of the iceberg and senior positions above you may be involved, we shall see," Dr. Burrows said.

"Now, start talking before I shove that inkwell right up your nose!" Harry demanded.

"Start talking before I crush your balls!" Olga said.

"You won't get away with this," Dr. Fellows pleaded.

"Yes, I will the CIA always gets its way. Now, spill the beans before I let Olga crush your balls. You'll squeal like a pig you are," Harry said, smiling.

Suddenly, Harry wasted no time in grabbing Dr. Fellows by his shirt collar and threw him across the room. Within seconds, the doctor was willing to spill the beans. The doctor started by saying he was only doing it for the extra money, which in Africa went a long way. Dr. Fellows said he played no part in any of the outbreaks, and that he only took advantage of the chaos this caused in the country by selling certain drugs on the black market.

Dr. Fellows said the new drug Dexamethasone was widely sought after on the black market because it was used to treat a wide range of medical conditions. He explained that the health service in Mozambique was underfunded and some of the people involved with its administration were corrupt. He went on to stress that he had no involvement in the outbreaks in Mozambique and his only criminal act was his dealing in drugs on the black market in the country.

"How did you perpetuate your drug dealing on the black market?" Harry asked.

"I sold the extra units of Dexamethasone not used or needed for the Ebola outbreaks. No patients suffered because of my actions. All outbreaks had sufficient drugs to meet their needs at all times," Dr. Fellows replied.

"How much were you making on your sales of Dexamethasone?" Dr. Burrows asked.

"Well, because of the scarcity of the drug almost twice the retail price on the black market. I did it once, and then I got greedy and carried on," Dr. Fellows replied.

"Your first mistake was to believe you could cheat the system. Don't you know that fate always plays its hands when least expected? The situation of the Ebola outbreaks presented itself to you and instead of helping in the crisis, you chose to take the devil's path. You thought a few spare units of Dexamethasone I can make some extra money and nobody will miss it. And then, you couldn't help yourself. You were gradually sucked into a vortex of lies and fraud to keep the money coming. You were 'all in' as they say in poker. Didn't your parents tell you that crime doesn't pay? You've just ruined a good career, and now you will need to find redemption, otherwise, you won't be going to heaven," Olga said solemnly.

"Well said! I would add that it's not our job to seek justice for you that's down to the local police force. Our job was to find out what was going on here in Mozambique concerning the Ebola outbreaks and I think we now have a clearer picture of what's been happening here. It's like I said from the beginning, a massive fraud. The Ebola problem is now something Olga, Dr Burrows and I need to discuss privately. In the meantime, we will wait until the police get here and then hand you over to them," Harry said.

***

Later, at the bar in their hotel, they sat discussing how to proceed further with the case. They all felt there was more to the case than the fraud committed by Dr. Fellows. They did not know how far into the WHO organisation the conspiracy had perpetrated. They now considered it to be a conspiracy perpetrated by persons unknown at present. Harry explained the need to go to its United Nations (UN) headquarters and find the answers there.

"I think, we're all wrapped up here, so in the morning, I'm on my way home first flight out of here, if the Learjet is not available," Harry said as he bought a round of drinks. And he was already thinking about seeing his sister for a well-earned holiday.

"Copy that," Dr. Burrows said.

"Well, I've made my report and sent it off. It's now up to my boss and his decision to pursue it further. What about you, Olga?" Harry asked.

"Much the same, but I may have stressed my opinions too much, rather than stick to the facts, which in this case is as elusive as a virgin in a brothel," Olga replied, smiling.

"What about you John?" Harry asked nonchalantly.

"I will make out a report and send it as soon as I get back to the jungle. I can only list the circumstantial evidence and what my conclusions are. It's then up to my employers to do with it what they want. They won't be happy about losing the Cessna, but that's the cost of doing business," Dr. Burrows replied.

***

Back at CIA headquarters in Langley, Virginia on the third floor stood Harry Steel in front of his boss Michael Kurios Director of Counter Intelligence. Harry was waiting to give his report of his findings out in Mozambique when his boss had finished speaking on the phone. Harry gazed at the river in the distance and wondered how to frame his verbal report. In his written report he had kept to the facts like every other report he had previously written thereby keeping his thoughts and often his conclusions to himself. It was the time for the same treatment, he said to himself.

"Hi Harry, sorry for the delay, how's it going?" Michael Kurios asked.

"Okay, sir, I'm fine."

"Good, what news do you have about Mozambique?" Michael asked.

"We uncovered fraud and theft from the WHO by the head honcho in Mozambique a Dr. Fellows. The rest of my verbal report consists of circumstantial evidence. There seems to be a pattern to the Ebola outbreaks when there shouldn't be one. Dr. Olga Domleic, Dr. John Burrows and I all agree that to be the case. Also, there's the case of Dengue Fever, which is normally only found up north in the Arabian countries and not down south in Mozambique. Apparently, the Aedes mosquito doesn't normally live that far south, which is suspicious or just a coincidence. You know how I feel about coincidences they're not normally at play. And the pattern of Ebola outbreaks suggests human hands have an involvement in the pattern and distribution throughout Mozambique. I suggest in my report that further investigation is required at the UN headquarters of the WHO to see who's involved. Olga,

Dr. Burrows and I all feel a massive fraud is taking place, but like I said we only have circumstantial evidence," Harry explained.

"Well, you could be right, but I understand you're about to take a holiday?" Michael asked.

"Yeah, I need some rest and relaxation," Harry replied.

"Good, have your holiday and I'll see you after and decide what's next then," Michael said.

Michael watched as Harry made his way out of the office and Michael thought about how close Harry's conclusions were to the actual truth. Michael had held back the truth right from the beginning of the mission and knew his agent was right on the money. He did not like to keep the truth from Harry, but for now, it was the only thing he could do without letting the cat out of the bag, he said to himself.

***

Later that day, inside the secure room all the section chiefs had gathered to hear the latest news from Michael Kurios. Paul Henderson Director of the CIA with access to the president of the United States sat at the head of the table as those gathered waited for the meeting to start.

"Good afternoon ladies and gentlemen, we're gathered here today to hear the latest update from Michael," Paul Henderson Director of the CIA said.

"Thank you, you'll see a copy of the report in front of you, which I received this morning from my agent Harry Steel concerning events in Mozambique. You will notice that it only deals with the facts of the case as they stand. My agent also gave me a verbal report outlining the circumstantial evidence of the case. Dr. Olga Domleic, Dr. John Burrows and my agent all believe a massive fraud is taking place by persons unknown and have classed it as a conspiracy within the WHO organisation. They've seen a pattern to the Ebola outbreaks when there shouldn't be one. They're also suspicious about an outbreak of Dengue Fever, again there shouldn't be one. They assume a conspiracy within the WHO and noted it needs further investigation as a course of action. Well, we all know they're right on the money, but the truth stays within this room for now," Michael said.

"Thank you, Michael. Are there any thoughts on the matter?" Paul Henderson asked.

"Do you plan to send your agent back in to investigate the WHO at the UN?" Ruth Gillingham Director of Internal Affairs asked.

"No, he's on holiday for a few days and will be reassigned when he gets back from holiday. As you know there's no point in chasing a horse when it's already bolted down the racecourse," Michael replied, smiling.

"How long do we have to keep this charade going, sooner or later the truth is bound to seep out like water from a leaky bucket?" Anthony Pagilia Director of Espionage asked.

"Whatever we do we have to keep the truth until we're ready!" Paul Henderson stated. Continuing, he added, "Have you something to add, Ruth?"

"Yes, thank you, Paul. What will happen, Michael if your agent finds out the truth before we're ready to reveal it?" Ruth Gillingham Director of Internal Affairs asked.

"He's one of my top agents and will keep his secret like all the other secrets he knows… it's part of his job…you know that," Michael replied annoyingly.

"Any more questions for Michael?" Paul Henderson asked.

"When do you think we will be ready, Paul?" Julia Hayward Director of Special Operations asked.

"That's a question for the general," Paul Henderson replied.

"Perhaps, two years from now or maybe never, our abilities are governed by how fast we can incorporate new technology into our weapons arsenal. We're working as fast as we can safely go. We have to match at least the enemies' firepower; otherwise, we risk losing before we've even fired the first shot," General John Schneider Director of Operations said.

"Are there any more questions or thoughts?" Paul Henderson asked as he looked around the table at his directors.

"Yes, do we know how safe the secret is in the president's circle?" George Hammond Director of Communications asked.

"Yes, we're keeping an eye on that situation, as we speak. The president and two others know the secret and this will be maintained or we may have to intervene," Paul Henderson replied knowing that any breach in the president's circle would require immediate action. Everyone gathered at the table knew what would likely happen.

***

Later that day, Paul Henderson was on his way in his chauffer driven car towards the White House to see the president. As he walked along the corridor from the rear of the White House he passed painting after painting of past presidents before he was at the Oval Office. On entering the room he saw the president discussing recent poll results concerning the upcoming election race with some of his advisors. The president noticed his Secretary of State and his Chief of Staff arrive for the briefing with Paul Henderson. The president dismissed his other advisors for the briefing with the CIA Director.

"Good afternoon Mr President, I have the latest news from Mozambique. You have the report in front of you, but it doesn't contain all the information we currently have.

"Thank you, Paul, please go ahead and give me a verbal brief of the situation as it stands," the president asked.

"Yes, of course. Our agent Harry Steel and our asset Dr. John Burrows and our Russian help Dr. Olga Domlieic believe a massive fraud is taking place. They believe a conspiracy of persons unknown within the WHO organisation is responsible for the Ebola outbreaks in Mozambique. They detected a pattern in the Ebola outbreaks when there shouldn't be one. Plus an outbreak of Dengue Fever is another outbreak in Mozambique when there shouldn't be one due to the fact that normally the mosquito that spreads the virus is normally found farther north in the Arabian countries. So, we're certain that our enemies have perpetrated these attacks on Mozambique as you are well aware of Mr President," Paul Henderson said.

"Does your agent know the truth?" the president asked.

"No, they believe that persons unknown within the WHO organisation are responsible for the Ebola and Dengue Fever outbreaks," Paul Henderson replied. Continuing, he added, "They have no idea of the truth."

"Good, we need to keep it that way until we're ready to fight back. When does that day arrive?" the president asked.

"General Schneider believes around two years or never. He outlined the problem as being able to adapt new technology into our weapons arsenal. He said they are going as fast as they can safely go. He said they don't want to attack without being at least on a level playing field or they could lose the war before they've fired the first shot. As you know our increased military spending is due to the need to be ready as we can be when an attack comes. In the meantime, it's important not to alarm the enemy before we're ready to fight back," Paul Henderson replied.

"Are we certain it's our enemy conducting these virus attacks?" Felix Gardner Chief of Staff asked.

"Yes, absolutely no doubt about it," Paul Henderson replied.

"Do we know why they are conducting these attacks?" Jerry Lauder Secretary of State asked.

"We've ideas and theories as to why they are conducting these attacks, but no sound evidence as to why," Paul Henderson replied.

"What is your view, Paul," the president asked.

"To be perfectly honest I've no idea and I don't like to speculate because speculation can cost lives," Paul Henderson replied.

"You must have a view, Paul," Jerry Lauder Secretary of State asked.

Paul Henderson grimaced at the thought of giving an answer to a question that had racked his brain since the very start of the outbreaks around the world. He knew his colleagues expected an answer, but he did not have one. All that mattered was to keep the truth from the public because he feared total anarchy should the truth get out before the armed forces were ready, he thought.

"In my view, they're trying to destabilise our society before they attack in full," Paul Henderson replied. Continuing, he added, "But, I could be completely wrong, that's why I don't like assumptions or speculation."

"Well, at least, we have got an idea what's going around in your brain Paul," the president said.

"Wasn't it Sun Tzu in the 'art of war' who said the easiest way to conquer a country was to divide it first?" Felix Gardner Chief of Staff asked.

"Yes, it was and they're probably doing the same, but on a larger scale," Paul Henderson replied.

"What will happen if I don't get elected for another term Paul?" the president asked.

"Nothing, you three will have to keep the secret and the new president and his closest advisors will be informed of the situation. Standard procedure for any outgoing president and his staff who have been privy to state secrets," Paul Henderson explained. Continuing, he added, "There're will be consequences for anyone breaking their silence."

It was anyone's guess what the CIA would do to those who broke their silence on the matter. It could involve assassination to a freak accident anything was possible. The CIA were past masters at the art of keeping secrets under lock and key and no one should be surprised at what the CIA were willing to do. Paul Henderson knew how important the truth was and how much the CIA would go to keep it that way, he said to himself.

"Are there any more questions?" the president asked.

The President looked at his advisors and Paul and saw no reaction and was preparing to end the meeting when he suddenly thought about asking what Paul was doing on the weekend.

"Paul, what plans have you for the weekend?" the president asked.

"I was planning to spend the weekend up in the

Appalachian Mountains in my cabin with the family, and you Mr President?" Paul Henderson asked.

"I plan some golf in Florida and to work on my tan," the president said, laughing.

***

On the drive back from Langley, Virginia, Paul wondered why the president asked about his plans for the weekend. He assumed the president wanted to know just in case he needed to find him for something. But, he was not sure of the president's motives. He considered the president a difficult man to read and one where his finger was on the nuclear button, which frightened him, he thought.

Chapter 7

The whole world was searching for answers ever since the Covid-19 pandemic had hit in the early part of the twenty-first century. The scientific community had been searching for cures and vaccines in a desperate attempt at saving the world from economic disaster and the increasing excessive death rate.

On a cold and windy day in late summer, Dr. Rebecca Steel was sat at her desk at home in Boston, Massachusetts busy reading the latest news from her friends in Africa. She was intrigued to hear about the latest Ebola outbreaks in Mozambique and felt sure something was amiss, but could not put her finger on it. Having worked in Rwanda as a forensic anthropologist dealing with the past genocide and mass graves, she had an affinity for the people and the continent of Africa. Now, back in her home state and teaching at Boston University where she had previously gained a doctorate in forensic anthropology, she was eager to pursue her other passion, which was the research into paranormal events. She believed that reality and the paranormal were linked somehow, and it was her passion to solve that enigma if she could. Now, in her early thirties, she felt she had enough past experience of the dead to offer the world of the paranormal. The prospect of ghosts and ghouls did not frighten her; what she feared most was the thought of dying without understanding her calling in life. Suddenly, her mobile was ringing.

"Hello, Dr Rebecca Steel speaking."

"Hi, my name is Arthur Tiller, I understand from your ad posted in the Boston Herald that you are interested in paranormal events," Arthur Tiller said.

"Yes, that's correct."

"Well, there's something going on in this house,

which may be of interest to you. When can you come and investigate?" Arthur asked.

"Today, say about twelve this afternoon, would that suit you?"

"Yes, that's fine. The address is forty-two Barclay Avenue, close to the old port docks on the east side of the town," Arthur replied.

***

Later that day, Dr. Rebecca Steel was on her way to meet Arthur Tiller at his home situated close to the old port dock area. Driving along the road that led to the port area, Rebecca noticed much of the port buildings were in disrepair with many buildings boarded up and were no longer functioning entities. The long-awaited refurbishment of the area into upmarket warehouse apartments was long overdue, she thought.

Looking at the house she saw the building had probably been constructed during the early part of the nineteenth century. The rambling wooden detached house needed overdue repairs and repainting and the surrounding gardens and apple trees also needed urgent attention to clear the overgrown weeds and shrubs. Rebecca climbed the steps to the porch and knocked on the front door, while she waited for an answer, she noticed the windows had no mosquito nets in place. She gazed at the rocking chair on the porch and it reminded her of her grandfather's house where she often stayed during summer breaks from school. Her grandfather would sit in his rocking chair and watch as she played in the garden. The door opened to the sound of a squeaky door hinge that needed oil, but just the same, it gave the atmosphere an eerie feel, she thought.

It was surprisingly dark as she entered the house at Arthur's gesture; yet, it was bright and sunny outside after the earlier wind and rain that morning. She could smell the years of dust that had accumulated over everything she could see. The mahogany and oak antique furniture that she could see had its own lingering smell.

"So, how can I help?" Dr. Rebecca Steel asked.

"There's a paranormal presence in this house!" the old man replied.

"How long have you lived here Mr Tiller?"

"All my life, I was born in this house…" the old man replied.

"How long have you had this paranormal experience in this house?" Rebecca asked.

"It started about three months ago. Before that I didn't notice anything out of the ordinary," the old man replied.

"And what exactly happens?"

"Things go flying through the air, and things fall over with no aid from the wind as I keep my windows and doors shut," the old man said.

"What time does this happen?" Rebecca asked calmly.

"Around three in the morning most times," the old man replied.

"Well, do you know the history of the house?"

"No, I don't."

"Good, I'll go back and do some research and return later is that alright with you?"

"Yes, that's fine, when will you return?" the old man asked.

"Around about two in the morning, so don't go to bed and wait for me to arrive and I may have a friend with me to help collect data, is that alright? Rebecca asked.

"Yes, that's fine, see you later," the old man said.

Rebecca felt a cold chill run up her back to her neck like a slithering snake as she walked outside to her car. Yet, the sun was shining and the day was warm in the afternoon sunshine, she thought. She wondered what history the house would reveal to her, perhaps the house was built on land where a Civil War battle took place. She knew Boston had a colourful history around the Civil War times. Boston had also been defended throughout the War of Independence by the British. In fact, Boston had been the flame that lit the torch of resistance to British rule and eventually started the War of Independence. The infamous Boston Tea Party where rioters boarded a cargo ship and threw a consignment of tea into the sea that was bound for England and other acts of discourse that led eventually to the signing of the Declaration of Independence, which was seen by the British as an act of treason. Rebecca knew the house was not that old and was probably built around the time of the Civil War, she said to herself.

Back home sat at her desk, Rebecca started to do some research on the Internet about the old man's house and the land it was built on. Looking at old maps of Boston she could see where the Civil War battles took place and saw the link to a massacre that happened during the war.

On a cold and wet morning in late November, during the first years of the Civil War prisoners were hanged from every tree in the apple orchard to discourage the opposition from fighting. Delving back further into the history of the area, Rebecca noticed that the British had slaughtered hundreds of captured colonists in the area where the house was eventually built. The British had massacred the colonists rather than deal with prisoners they had no means to feed and support. Rebecca now knew the history of the area and it was not unusual for paranormal events to be happening, but what she did not understand was why now, she said to herself.

· Arthur Tiller had said the paranormal events had started only three months ago and Rebecca was puzzled by this anomaly. She found this strange because from her experience paranormal events normally follow a predictable pattern. From past experience of the paranormal, this occurs when new people move into a haunted house and disturb the spirits or someone close dies and the spirit still lingers in the house wanting to communicate. As an anthropologist, she considered the whole process of communication an ancient art. It was like the mystery of crop circles where some were just plain hoaxes, but others were totally real and you could tell by how the crops were flattened not by a human hand at work. It was another unseen force that was at play trying to communicate a message. An analogy of this she considered was how two people who neither spoke the other's language would try to communicate with each other. They may try to draw shapes to convey their message or make gestures to one another. After all, body language was the oldest form of language long before sounds and words came into play, she said to herself.

Rebecca looked out the window of her top-floor apartment and saw the Atlantic Ocean waves breaking along the shoreline in the distance. The sea looked cold and uninviting its colour a dark blue and greyish pastiche with white streaks spectacled to the horizon like an image of white horses dancing amongst the waves. Drinking her coffee, she was puzzled in her mind about how fate played a part in her life like a friend who was always there when you thought about it, she said to herself. She could see the trees starting to sway in the wind and sensed a storm was on its way and saw a flock of birds heading inland to avoid a coming sea storm. It was a way nature had to communicate a message to those who cared to observe its splendour. The birds could sense a storm was on its way many hours before it actually arrived.

Feeling alone in the world since her parents had passed away she now had only her older brother to care about. And he was somewhere in Africa the last time they spoke on the phone. She knew what her brother did for a living and most of the time he never mentioned anything to do with his work. But, he had mentioned his trip to Africa, which was out of character for him because normally he never said a word about where he was going or what he was doing. It was though subconsciously he was trying to convey a message that for the first time it felt different for him somehow. Perhaps, he was worried about what he was doing and just needed the support from his sister at that particular moment in time, she was not sure, she said to herself.

***

"Are you ready for this paranormal experience?" Rebecca asked, cheerfully.

"Yes, I've got some devices to record sights and sounds, so we should be alright for tonight," Raymond Speer replied.

On the drive to Arthur Tiller's house, Rebecca and Raymond discussed how they would proceed once in Tiller's home. Rebecca told Raymond about the research she had done on the area where the house was located.

"With that much history of massacres and battles in the area then I'm not surprised it's now haunted," Raymond said gleefully.

"Yet, it only started three months ago, that's what the old man said to me, yesterday," Rebecca said matter-of-factly.

"Yes, that's strange," Raymond said intently.

As Rebecca drove up to the front of the house and parked the only light were the street lights which cast a shadow away from the house. A large willow tree at the front of the house cast an eerie shadow as it swayed in the wind and the noise of the tree's branches swaying added to the spookiness of the place.

"The house does look spooky, but then again it's nearly two in the morning and anything looks spooky at this time of the night," Raymond said regretfully.

When Rebecca and Raymond approached the old man's house they felt the full force of the cold wind wrap around them like they were in an underground tube tunnel. All kinds of dirt and dead leaves flew about them as they noticed the trees swaying and shaking in the fierce wind. Only a few miles away the sea storm was in its element with giant waves crashing along the shoreline. The old man's house looked deserted as they saw no lights on. They knocked and waited. The creaking door opened and the old man beckoned them inside.

"Hi, Mr Tiller this is Raymond a student of the paranormal who will assist me tonight," Rebecca said dutifully.

"I'll set up these remote cameras and sound devices around the house while we wait for the spooks to appear," Raymond said nonchalantly. He was sceptical about finding any paranormal events because from past experience with Rebecca on other haunts they usually came away empty-handed.

"Has anything occurred tonight?" Rebecca asked the old man.

"No, not so far, but one hopes they appear tonight," the old man said, grinning like a Cheshire cat, his teeth visible and stained with nicotine as he inhaled on his cigarette.

"I did some research on the house and the area, and it turns out that there's plenty of history. There were scenes of massacres and battles during the Civil War and the War of Independence, right in this location, so it may be related to that why you have experienced those paranormal events you told me about. But, why they only started three months ago is a mystery. Perhaps, tonight we will be wiser, who knows," Rebecca said pensively.

Rebecca gazed at the grandfather clock in the hallway as Raymond came down the stairs it was almost three in the morning. Raymond looked spooked as she saw his face was white as pure snow.

"I've placed all the devices and they're ready to record. I felt a cold chill in one of the bedrooms…it was like a feeling of dread and doom that came over me without warning. I saw nothing…but felt everything enter my body like I'd seen a ghost. It just drained me with a fear of foreboding. I can't explain it…it was a horrible feeling," Raymond explained.

"Well, that's what we're here for let's wait here in the living room and see what happens. Any noises you hear will probably be the wind outside affecting the house," Rebecca said.

Suddenly, they could hear the loud noise of what sounded like doors opening and shutting. Rebecca screamed as she felt a hand touch her right shoulder. Raymond felt a cold chill again enter his body and that it ran up from his toes to his head like a cold chill in winter. The old man Tiller watched as books started to fly across the room and furniture started to levitate and crash around them. All three of them ran to the basement door as a milky cloud appeared in the living room and began to surround them.

"Get down the basement!" the old man shouted.

In the basement, they could hear the commotion upstairs as they all huddled together near the heating boiler. They all gazed at the milky cloud that had followed them down into the basement and now swirled around them like they were caught in a whirlpool ready to suck them into an abyss. Old man Tiller cringed at what he saw and at times closed his eyes. Rebecca felt sick with pangs of stomach ache and Raymond looked as pale as a ghost.

"What do you want?" Rebecca shouted at the cloud as ghostly figures appeared and then disappeared into the white haze. No answer came.

Then suddenly, the noise from upstairs stopped and the white cloud vanished. Raymond winced as he felt his body return to normal and Rebecca no longer felt sick. And the old man opened his eyes and shrugged his shoulders.

"Are they gone?" the old man asked.

"Yes, I think so," Rebecca replied hopefully.

"Shit! That was scary; I really thought I was going to die. Well, that's what I felt. It was as though I was in the throes of hell. I've never experienced such a freighting and creepy place before this night. What does it all mean?" Raymond asked.

"Let's get back upstairs and see what we can find out," Rebecca said casually.

Looking around the living room they all saw the mess. Books lay all over the place and furniture lay turned upside down and ornaments smashed and scattered across the room. It was as if the place had been ransacked by burglars.

"Look for any clues to what we have just witnessed."

"Just what are we looking for?" Raymond asked pensively.

"Get your mobile out and take some pictures of everything you see," Rebecca demanded.

The old man stood shaking at what he could see and had just witnessed. Rebecca told him to sit down while they tried to make sense of the mess as she and Raymond began to clear up the room for the old man. Raymond took lots of photos just to make sure he had not missed something. The only sounds they could now hear were emanating from the house itself as it creaked from the raging storm outside.

"What are we trying to capture?" Raymond asked curiously.

"As I said before…I don't know, but I believe the paranormal events in this house are trying to tell us something. Well, at least, that's what I think. What else could it be? Think about the crop circle issue, we know some are pure hoaxes, but the majority have been scientifically proven to be real. This they have established by the stems of the plants and the way they have been thrashed down without any damage to the stems. We have scientific proof that this cannot be done by human hands. So, we have a dilemma and science has not provided any answers to what may have made the crop circles and what they mean."

Rebecca then explained to Raymond and old man Tiller what she thought about crop circles. She explained that those elaborate crop circle designs in her view were trying to convey a message to the world. If the crop circles were trying to warn us, then they have not done their job.

"What about the animal mutilations occurring across the world?" Raymond asked curiously. Continuing, he added, "Are they trying to convey a message?"

"No, I don't believe so, but then again I don't

have any proof to back up my assertion. From all the evidence, you can clearly see it wasn't wild animals that inflicted those injuries to those animals. Science has established the precision cuts and removal of organs requires sophisticated laser tools and experience. And the lack of blood present at the site of the dead animals leads one to conclude someone is experimenting with our livestock. Who and why we don't have answers, but something major is happening and the world is pretty calm about the problem," Rebecca said.

Rebecca and Raymond noticed the old man had stopped shaking and was now returning to normal.

"Remember, the 'mad cow' disease…they fed cows with dead cows? They fed herbivores with meat and this started the whole 'mad cow' disease," the old man muttered.

"He's getting better!"

"Yeah, I remember when they said it was safe to eat the meat, but we later found out it wasn't so safe, as people started to develop the human form of the disease," the old man said.

"When you fuck with nature it has a habit of biting you in the ass," Raymond said, smiling.

"They called it the Prion, which apparently is harder to kill than a ghost. It can take temperatures of three thousand degrees to kill it. Yet, they just buried the dead cows in pits which were lined with impregnable type plastics, so that the water table wasn't breached," the old man said.

"Shit! You know a lot about this," Raymond said.

"Had no choice, it's what we saw on television and what they told us on the news. It freaked out a lot of people. If you saw the images of cows and people who suddenly couldn't stand up without falling over, you'd be shocked. It shocked the nation," the old man said.

"Well, Mr Tiller you seemed to have recovered. What happened here tonight is truly a mystery. Your spirits are trying to convey a message to you. What that message is and why now is a mystery? Perhaps, we will know more when we have examined the recordings of tonight's events," Rebecca said.

"Yeah, the government then said not to worry the Prion may manifest itself in twenty or thirty years, they told us. Which is about now…and we see in dementia the biggest cause of death. You have to wonder about the possible link between the two," the old man said.

"Well, you seem fine…dementia hasn't caught you," Raymond said, smiling.

"That's because I never ate the meat back then. I didn't trust the government and was proved right when several months into the fiasco they admitted it probably wasn't safe to eat the meat. Shamefully, at the time, they even got a government minister's daughter to eat the meat. All the government were interested in was saving the meat industry at the time from collapse," the old man replied.

"Yes, well, you're right the government of the day keep lots of secrets from us…that's just the way it is. They don't trust us and assume we would all panic. I would like to be told the truth no matter what. Like for instance, what was going on in the minds of the astronauts who were first being interviewed after the first moon landings. They look like a bunch of miserable people, yet, you'd expect to see smiles and laughter on their faces. They've just come back from a historic mission and they look like they've been to a funeral. What was going on, because something clearly was going on? Those astronauts look like they're about to cry. It doesn't make sense," Rebecca said.

"Yeah, I've seen the same and they do look

miserable. That doesn't make sense. Every face conveys a message…that much you have shown me," the old man said.

"Whatever that message is…then I doubt whether our governments will inform us. They're too worried about the likely response and they would rather keep us chained to the job and paying the mortgage," Rebecca said.

"Eh, I like what you said. It's a revolution from the drudgery that so many people put up with. Whatever is happening it's been happening for some time," Raymond said.

"I'll call you when I think we have something. But, feel free to call me if you're having trouble coping. Perhaps, you could move out until this is all over. It's up to you. In the meantime, thanks again for letting us record your paranormal events," Rebecca said.

Rebecca and Raymond immediately noticed how calm it was outside. The raging storm had abated and now the sunshine shone through the early morning haze.

"I'll look through the recordings later today, I've got a couple of lectures to attend this afternoon at the university," Rebecca said.

"Yes, I've got to get back to working on my PhD; I'll call round later tonight and help you go through the recordings. Boy…that was a weird experience last night," Raymond stressed.

Chapter 8

On the drive up to Boston, Massachusetts to see his sister, Harry Steel was looking forward to a few days of relaxation. He wondered how his boss and the CIA would react to his report on the Ebola outbreaks in Mozambique. He wondered about his next mission. But, most of all he thought about seeing his sister.

"Hi, glad to see you, Rebecca…we haven't touched base for a while," Harry said.

"Come in…and let's celebrate with a few drinks before we eat," Rebecca said.

"So, how's it been…what are you up to these days?" Harry asked.

"I'm fine being busy at the university teaching and investigating paranormal events. You know I've had an interest in the paranormal, ever since I can remember. You know I'm like a kid in a sweet shop, I just love it," Rebecca replied. Continuing, she added, "So, what about you Harry are you okay?"

"Yes, you know me loving what life brings and say whatever happens…happens. Fate call it what you like, but when it plays its hands you can't go against it. And I can't talk about any of my missions. That's me in a nutshell," Harry replied, smiling.

"So, what are your plans?"

"Just to relax and enjoy your company," Harry said, smiling.

"Good, because tonight, I have got a paranormal event to attend to close by…near the old port end of Boston. So, if you want to get spooked then now's your opportunity, but, it's not until two in the morning."

"I will let you know nearer the time," Harry replied.

***

Later that night, Rebecca, Harry and Raymond set off for the old man Tiller's house the scene of the previous encounter with the paranormal. It was raining and a gusting wind ensued. The sound of the howling wind was like a recurring deep hum that almost spoke words. As the group walked up to the house they could see no lights were on. All the trees around the house were shaking and creaky as the squall caught the branches like a fishermen's net. The sound of their knocking on the front door was almost drowned out by the sound of the ferocious wind. Then old man Tiller beckoned them into a barely lit house.

"Mr Arthur Tiller this is Harry Steel my brother and of course you know Raymond," Rebecca said.

"Well, tonight we hope to try and make some sense of this paranormal activity for you.

"Hopefully, you won't feel frightened by events. Before we do that…Raymond is going to set some cameras about your home, okay," Rebecca said as Raymond started placing cameras in each room.

"Last time, we had activity around three in the morning, but it looks like it could get started any minute now.

"Whatever happens we hope to get the answers we have been looking for," Rebecca said amusingly.

"What answers are you looking for?" Harry asked.

"Mr Tiller said the paranormal events started around three months ago. Normally, events don't just start, unless something has upset the spirits somehow. We hope to understand what has caused this paranormal event to occur. Mr Tiller said that he has lived in the house all his life except for a brief spell in England when he was in the forces and he hasn't experienced any paranormal events before three months ago. So, the enigma is why now? We believe that the spirits are trying to convey a message to Mr Tiller. Hopefully, we can understand that message so that Mr Tiller can live in the house peacefully. Well, that's the plan," Rebecca said.

"I've set all the cameras around the house, so we're ready as can be," Raymond said.

"Good, all we can do now is wait and see what happens," Rebecca said with a soft tone of voice.

All four of them sat waiting in the old man's living room. The only noise they could hear was the creaking of timber as the storm outside continued to rage. At times they could hear the howling wind as it battered the house from all sides. The rain continued to hit the windows in a continuous wave as it sounded like someone knocking on the front door relentlessly. Harry felt relaxed and almost fell asleep waiting for the spirits to make their presence.

"Did you hear that…doors slamming shut?"

They could hear pots and pans crashing to the kitchen floor and then they saw books and ornaments flying across the living room before ending up on the floor. Harry did not know what to believe he had never witnessed anything like it before. They all saw the white misty cloud appear as it circled the room moving objects and furniture with ease around them. Raymond felt the hair on the back of his neck stand up straight and he winced at the feeling he had. Rebecca also felt the hair on her neck curl up at the sight she could see. The old man looked again pale and frightened at what he could see. Harry watched the misty cloud with feelings of contempt for what he was witnessing and had doubts about the paranormal event.

"What do you want?" Rebecca shouted. She was not sure what to say, but needed answers, if only for Mr Tiller's sanity. No answer came from the misty white cloud as it continued to circle them and move them about in their seats with ease.

"What do you want?" Rebecca shouted again.

Occasionally, a face would briefly appear in the cloud and then disappear just as quickly. The noise from the raging storm outside and the clatter of doors shutting and furniture scraping across the wooden floors added to the noise of rain rattling at the windows. It was a cacophony of sounds all mixing together to perform a crescendo for all to hear.

"What do you want?" Rebecca shouted again anxiously.

Suddenly, the old man was lifted out of his seat and suspended in the air for a few seconds and then dumped down into his seat. Raymond felt that cold chill he had previously experienced run up his body like an ill chill in winter. He felt as though his body was being taken over with pangs of sickness envelope his stomach like before, he thought. Rebecca had the same misgivings as before with the feelings of doom wretch her body as she fought to repel the sensation. Harry felt the horror drain his face like feeling a tsunami was coming without being able to stop it; he was totally helpless, he said to himself.

"What the fuck do you want?" Harry howled out aggressively.

Within minutes, as suddenly as it started all the commotion stopped and there on the table they all saw the pages of a book turn over and stop as well. Harry was the first one to notice the book was the Bible and the place where it had stopped.

"Let me see, Harry!"

"It's a message…it's what we've been looking for," Rebecca said.

"What does it say?" the old man asked.

"It's from the book of the Ecclesiastes."

"Let me read it out loud?" Raymond asked.

"No, we will go away and study it and return with an answer for Mr Tiller," Rebecca said.

"Will you be alright, Mr Tiller?" Harry asked. He could see the old man trembling as he spoke.

"Yes, I'm fine…just a little shaken up that's all," the old man replied.

"Raymond can you take some photos and collect our cameras," Rebecca said.

"Yes, will do."

"Here I've made you a cup of coffee, Mr Tiller," Rebecca said.

"What happens next?" Harry asked.

"We'll go away after Mr Tiller is okay and then review our recordings and the Bible pages and figure out what it all means. Hopefully, we can now provide Mr Tiller with some answers and he can get back to his life as it was before."

"I remember Sunday school like it was yesterday. The book of Ecclesiastes is about wisdom and the fear of God and that all life is meaningless, is that right?" Harry asked.

"Yes, you're right…but I think a bit more than just that Harry," Rebecca said.

"Yeah, I believe it's more than that," Raymond agreed.

"It's about the 'march of time' and that we've no control of that or indeed our lives. We may think we've control of our lives, but chance plays its part where random events happen good or bad which steer us in a different direction. Like I said we've no control over our lives. I like to think about the fate of that unseen force, which plays its hand when least expected. Fate is probably just another word for chance. We can't predict it, but it's there ready and waiting to steer our course. Then, of course, there's greed, when a man succumbs to greed he's then on the slippery road to disaster. Many a philosopher has spoken about how greed has a way of sinking the ship before you've had a chance to jump off," Harry said philosophically.

"I didn't realise you could be so metaphysical," Rebecca said, smiling.

"I probably read too much," Harry said.

"No, you're right Harry. Chance is a great leveller, which catches most people when they're not looking," Raymond said.

***

On the way back to Rebecca's home they noticed the storm had subsided and now the sun had started to shine through the early morning mist.

"What a night! The paranormal is certainly strange."

"The old man was again going on about the outbreak of 'mad cow' disease," Raymond said.

"Yeah, I can remember that outbreak, it was the year you were born, Rebecca," Harry said. Continuing, he added, "It started in nineteen eighty-six. And the first cases of the human form of the disease were detected in the mid-nineties."

"Yes, that's right from what I've read about the outbreak it was very serious and started in England. Long before you were born Raymond," Rebecca said.

"The old man mentioned something about a Prion; I'll have to look that up. At the time, I paid no attention to the outbreak because it was in England and not here. I was a teenager at the time and had other things on my mind like girls," Harry said, smiling.

***

"Well, for now, let's review the camera footage

and see what we have," Rebecca said.

"Shit! Did you see that?" Raymond asked.

"Yes, it's what we expected to see, we heard the sound of doors shutting from downstairs. Look for anything that seems out of place. What that would be, I'm not sure," Rebecca said.

"I'm amazed at the noise of the paranormal event," Raymond said.

"Yes, that's because when you're in the moment your ears have a tendency to block out some of the noise and your brain then locks on to certain criteria," Rebecca said.

"Look! There's the white cloud starting to appear from the basement floor and rise up the steps and into the living room like it knew where we were. Whatever it is…it's certainly spooky," Raymond said.

"What are we looking for?" Harry asked.

"Anything that can solve this mystery for Mr Tiller would be useful. Freeze that and go back a few frames, Raymond," Rebecca asked as she thought she saw a face appear.

"It's a face, but it only appears for a fleeting moment," Raymond said.

"Take a screenshot and we'll blow up the image and see if we can get a better look at the face. Let's continue on."

"There again the face appears, stop the footage and go back a few frames and capture the image of the face and compare again," Rebecca said.

"Does it trigger any thoughts on who it may be?" Harry asked.

"Not me."

"Nor me," Raymond agreed.

After several hours of reviewing the cameras' footage, they were all exhausted from their efforts and had a night without sleep. Raymond went home. Rebecca decided to get some sleep, while Harry was wide awake and was busy researching on Google the book of Ecclesiastes. He was intrigued to find the message if there was one. Later that day, Harry showed Rebecca what he had found from the Bible page that was shown to them in the old man's house.

"This statement seems to be relevant, "Whatever exists is far off and most profound— who can discover it?" Harry said.

"I'll spend some time reading the section of the book of Ecclesiastes later today," Rebecca said.

"It's hard to figure out what it means, but I feel sure this may be a clue," Harry said.

"You best get some sleep, before you keel over and die on me Harry," Rebecca said, smiling.

***

Inside the Kremlin, Alexi Polokov Chief of Secret Intelligence Service stood to attention opposite the President of Russia waiting for the president to finish his phone call.

"Take a seat, Alexi," the president demanded.

"Thank you, Mr President."

"What news do you have for me?" the president asked.

"Our agent Dr. Olga Domlieic has just returned from Mozambique and a full report is on your desk in front of you," Polokov replied.

"Yes, I can see it, but I want a verbal report from you comrade," the president said.

"Our agent, Dr. Olga Domlieic with the help of the CIA believes a massive fraud is taking place by persons unknown within the WHO organisation based in its headquarters at the United Nations (UN) in New York. They also uncovered a small scale fraud based in

Mozambique, which is being dealt with by the local police force. Our agent saw a pattern in the Ebola outbreaks when there shouldn't be one, which first alerted their attentions to a conspiracy taking place. There was also an outbreak of Dengue Fever when there shouldn't be one, because the female mosquito that carries the virus normally lives in the Arabian countries and not that far south in Mozambique. This outbreak of Dengue Fever was another anomaly that alerted the trio to the plausibility of a conspiracy. And...," Polokov said before being interrupted by the president.

"You said the trio, who's that comrade Polokov?" the president asked.

"Yes, our agent, Dr. Olga Domleic and the CIA agent Harry Steel and Dr. John Burrows another CIA asset."

"Continue."

"And they are none the wiser to the real truth, but we're sure the outbreaks are by the hands of our enemy. To what purpose we're not sure, perhaps, to destabilise the world. As you know only a few people within our government know the real truth and until the Americans and we are ready to fight back we have to keep it that way," Polokov said.

"Do we have effective quarantine procedures in place to stop the spread of Ebola reaching here?" the president asked.

"Yes, we're currently screening every one of our soldiers and personnel that return from Mozambique before they leave for Russia. And when they arrive here they are quarantined for another two weeks just to make sure we catch any possible spread of the virus. And over the last couple of years we now know a lot more about the virus and what works to save lives," Polokov said.

"What about the inquiry into the Covid-19

pandemic, how's that progressing?" the president asked.

"Current thinking and what has been revealed so far suggests it wasn't an accident on the part of the Chinese. It's more like they were the fall guys. Our scientists have analysed the genome of the virus and have concluded without doubt that it was manufactured in a laboratory somewhere. Without the cooperation of the Chinese we don't know if they played a part for our enemy," Polokov said.

"Okay, comrade Polokov, keep me informed should anything change," the president said as he watched his minister salute and leave the room.

***

Later that day, Harry Steel awoke on the couch to hear the sound of his sister Rebecca and Raymond discussing the previous night's events in the kitchen.

"You had a good sleep, Harry?" Rebecca asked.

"Yes, slept like a baby," Harry replied.

"Good, I've read the book of Ecclesiastes and studied the pages opened in the Bible and have come to some conclusions. Raymond and I were just discussing them when you woke up," Rebecca said.

"Yes, let's hear them," Harry said.

"Well, the book of Ecclesiastes is a book of wisdom written supposedly by King Solomon. Ecclesiastes is referred to as the teacher and the author as King Solomon both are most likely the same person. The book is constructed this way so that there are two voices speaking to the reader. This allows the reader to develop their own view governed by what the teacher has said and how the author sums up the issues. Now, I've studied the pages that were opened in the Bible and have found what I believe to be what the spirits wanted us to understand. This statement in the book "There is no remembrance of former things; neither shall there be any remembrance of things that are to come with those that shall come after" is I believe the essence of what they want us to understand?" Rebecca asked.

"An interesting observation, but I'm not sure what we're meant to understand," Raymond said.

"I've had the same doubts," Harry said. Continuing, he added, "Whatever exists is far off and most profound— who can discover it?" was the statement I found on the pages opened in the Bible and this I believe could be a clue."

"Harry, you're meant to be relaxing not working."

"After what I've experienced last night I'm intrigued to find out what's going on," Harry said.

"What baffles me is why the paranormal events started just three months ago? Rebecca asked.

Rebecca continued to explain to Harry the information surrounding the paranormal events. She explained that during the War of Independence the apple orchard where the house currently stands was where the British had hanged many prisoners of war. They did this as a warning to the rebels, which only served to strengthen the resolve of the rebels to continue their fight. She went on to explain how Mr. Tiller had been born in the house and had never previously experienced any paranormal events until it started three months ago.

"I don't know if this is anything to do with it, but there have been a lot of paranormal events happening…more than usual if that means something," Rebecca said.

"Yes, I've had the same feelings and it started around three months ago as if it meant something," Raymond said.

"I've had another call for tonight to a house in the same area, are you up for it Harry?" Rebecca asked.

"Yes, why not it beats watching TV," Harry replied.

"I'll see you around eight then," Raymond said before leaving the apartment.

***

Later that afternoon, Rebecca and Harry had a meal together and discussed life in general. Rebecca was keen to explain to Harry how much she enjoyed her job as an anthropologist and teaching at the university. She told Harry that she also enjoyed her role as a paranormal investigator and considered it a hobby. She explained that since the breakup of her last relationship she had found it difficult to meet another suitable man.

"I've had the same issues since my divorce to Angela; it's not easy when I'm hardly ever at home. The hobby I've got is watching the river pass my place in the Appalachians and the wildlife I see around it," Harry said.

"Oh, and reading…"

Rebecca continued to explain her life as an anthropologist, which she told Harry is the study of any organism and her field of study entailed the forensic study of man. She explained that her particular speciality was the study of humans and their bones and how they lived and died. She told Harry about her time in Africa examining mass graves of the massacre of people during Rwanda's genocide.

"It was shocking to see so many skeletons stacked like rows of bottles as if in a wine rack."

Rebecca then continued to explain why the genocide occurred. "There were too many people with just hate in their bellies willing to kill without feelings." She then told him about the "special event theory" which many leading scientists and anthropologists had postulated may have happened in the past.

"Have you heard about the 'special event theory', Harry?" Rebecca asked with a soft tone of voice.

"Yes, but go ahead."

She explained that around forty thousand to fifty thousand years ago man started to paint on wall caves. And that man also started to develop sophisticated tools around this time. And it is assumed man also developed the ability to speak in a language that was understood. The leading scientists and anthropologists think a special event must have taken place at this time.

"That's the nuts and bolts of the theory."

"What was the event that changed everything?" Harry asked.

"They don't know for sure. But they say an event happened because we went from using the same flint tools that had been used for at least a million years to fashioning sophisticated wooden tools for the killing of prey, all this happened around fifty thousand years ago. Now, why is that?" Rebecca asked.

Rebecca explained that the "special event theory" went against the established Darwinian view of evolution. Essentially, small changes over a long period of time like millions of years are how Darwin explained his theory of evolution. She told Harry, that this irreconcilable difference should not be there.

"So, the logic goes that a special event must have occurred," Rebecca stressed.

"What do you think, Rebecca?"

"If you look at the time this occurred and correlate it to an event that happened on earth when we were struck by a wave of energy from a nearby star. We were hit with a form of radiation that would cause mutations in our DNA to occur more frequently than expected. This is in my view a special event. Other scientists have similar views as mine." Continuing, she added, "There are those that think aliens had a hand in changing our evolution. It's a possibility and I haven't discounted it, but I feel it's more likely to be an event, which we know occurred when this planet was hit with a high dose of radiation by the explosion of a nearby star. Radiation kills and mutates living organisms. We use radiation to kill cancer cells for patients with cancer. Any living organism around when this dose of high energy radiation hit our planet would have been affected."

"Sounds, plausible to me," Harry said.

Rebecca could hear a dog barking outside the apartment and wondered if Raymond had arrived.

"Hi, Raymond I heard the dog barking."

"Yes, he's your personal guard," Raymond said, laughing.

"Tonight, we've another caller in the same area as last night's event," Rebecca said.

Rebecca explained to Harry and Raymond that the house was up for sale but the present owner felt it was haunted and wanted Rebecca to investigate. As the trio approached the house they noticed the house was surrounded by the edge of the nearby forest. The only light was from the street lamp which was nearby. They shone their torches at the front door and unlocked the door with the key the owner had given Rebecca the day before. The house was all on one level as they entered the hallway to the building. They began to search each room which were empty except for the occasional pieces of furniture which had been covered over with white sheets. A few builders' tools were scattered across the floors in each room as if someone had been trying to make repairs to the house. Then Raymond thought he saw something from the corner of his right eye.

"Did you see that? A dark figure just darted across into the room at the end of the hallway,"

Raymond said.

"No, didn't see anything," Rebecca replied.

"No, I didn't see anything," Harry said.

"Go take a look in the room and shine your light around there, Raymond," Rebecca suggested.

"Perhaps, it's just a homeless person and we've disturbed them," Harry remarked.

Carefully, Raymond entered the room and saw nothing but covered furniture and empty cardboard boxes in the corner of the room. He tried to shine his torch into the shadows but saw no figure of a person. Satisfied no one was hiding in the room, Raymond closed the door of the room and joined Rebecca and Harry with the search through the rest of the house. As they entered the kitchen they noticed all the cupboards were empty of food except all the pots and pans still hung about the walls and the kitchen cutlery was neatly placed in the kitchen cupboard draws. A few builder's tools were strewn across the floor as if someone had been there trying to make repairs.

"If a homeless person is living here then there not using the kitchen," Harry said nonchalantly.

Suddenly, they heard a loud banging noise coming from another room off the hallway. They saw the door to the room violently shaking as if someone was banging against the door from inside the room. They stood outside the room and shouted out to the person or persons behind the door to stop and leave the property. But still, the door shook and the banging continued. Raymond then grabbed hold of the door handle and was ready with a knife in one hand to open the door. As Raymond pushed the door open as the banging noise stopped suddenly, but he saw no one. In one corner of the room, he shined his torch at the cardboard boxes stacked against a bed and saw nothing. Turning to see behind the door he saw a plaque on the floor which read "Go far from here and never come back," which he then placed back on its hanging. When Raymond went to leave the room he was caught from behind and an unseen force was now trying to pull Raymond back into the room.

"It's got me!" Raymond howled. His face was now contorted with fear.

"Something got me…"

Harry grabbed hold of Raymond and pulled against whatever was pulling at Raymond but saw no one. Within seconds, Raymond was free and standing in the hallway feeling injured. Harry and Rebecca saw the three deep cuts that ran down diagonally down from his shoulder to his right thigh as Raymond held up his shirt and jacket. The cuts looked like they had been done with a gardening fork slashing at his back.

"Where's my knife? I've dropped it in that room," Raymond said anxiously.

When Raymond entered the room again he saw his knife stuck into the wall. The knife had been rammed into the wall with such a force that the blade was buried deep into the wall right up to the handle guard. It took all of Raymond's strength to pull the knife from the wall. Harry and Rebecca watched from the doorway as Raymond quickly exited the room and closed the door.

"You saw the knife buried in the wall, it's a sign for us to get the hell out of here," Raymond insisted.

"We saw no sign of anyone in the room," Rebecca said.

"But, I felt a deep fear of dread as I entered this property, something I've never experienced before," Harry said.

"Why didn't you mention it before?" Raymond asked bluntly.

"I didn't want to spook anyone, just in case this property is haunted," Harry replied.

"After what I've experienced then this place is haunted with a demon," Raymond said.

"Yes, you're right, let's get the hell out of here before we regret it," Rebecca said.

As they emerged from the property they could hear the noise again of the doors banging inside. Rebecca told Harry and Raymond that the place needed an exorcist to rid the property of the demonic presence. Raymond's face had lost its colour and he looked as pale as a ghost. Harry felt the dread that had come over him drain away as he walked to the car.

"I'm not going back, that's for sure," Raymond said.

"What about you, Harry?" Rebecca asked.

"Only if you insist Rebecca, but to be honest I've had enough of the paranormal to last me the rest of my days," Harry replied exhausted.

"No, I'll tell the owner what we found and advise her to get an exorcist. I don't fancy going back in there without support," Rebecca said.

On the way back to Rebecca's apartment Raymond was still shaking from his experience and trembling over every word as he tried to speak. Harry recognised the signs of delayed shock within Raymond and wondered if the boy had been previously been this shaken up before. Harry was okay, he was used to shock and awe it was part of his daily life, but felt he had seen enough of the paranormal and was now convinced of its reality.

"I plan to spend the rest of my holiday relaxing and not ghost hunting," Harry said nonchalantly.

"Here's a cup of coffee, Raymond. You need to calm down and relax before you head home," Rebecca suggested.

"Thanks, I need to forget what just happened or it will haunt me forever," Raymond said muttering over each word as he still trembled throughout his body.

"Take your shirt off and let me clean your wounds," Rebecca demanded.

"Whatever that thing was it certainly made its mark on you. I can't believe what I'm seeing. You may need to go to the hospital. What do you think Harry?" Rebecca asked. She knew Harry would know what best to do.

"Yes, I think we should take him to the hospital those cuts look too deep to handle here," Harry suggested.

***

At the hospital, Harry asked the doctor to take a DNA sample from Raymond's cuts to see what it revealed. The doctor and nurse could not believe how Raymond had sustained the cuts to his body without his shirt being shredded in the process. There were three diagonal cuts spaced around an inch and a half apart, running from his left shoulder to his right thigh like he had been attacked and sliced with a garden fork. Harry and Rebecca explained to the doctor that they had been investigating a paranormal occurrence in a property when Raymond was attacked by an unseen force. The doctor looked on with disbelief as they tried to explain the circumstances of Raymond's injuries. It was only after Raymond had concurred with Harry and Rebecca's statement was the doctor satisfied everything was above board. Harry flashed his CIA credentials and insisted the doctor take DNA samples for further investigation and for the results to be sent to Rebecca's home address as soon as possible. Harry was intrigued to find out the results before he returned to work the following week.

They dropped Raymond off at his home before they drove back to Rebecca's apartment. Raymond was still shaking from his ordeal and they felt he should not drive while he was still in shock.

The neighbour's dog was barking as Rebecca and Harry entered the apartment complex.

"Now that we're alone and can relax and talk, are you really thinking of going back to that demonic place?" Harry asked. He did not like to think his sister would go alone without her sidekick Raymond.

"Yes, if I can get an exorcist to do the job. You're not afraid are you Harry?" Rebecca asked.

"You saw what it did to Raymond, doesn't that put you off?" Harry asked.

"You didn't answer my question."

"No, of course, I'm not afraid. Shit! Every time I go on a mission I'd be shitting my pants otherwise sis," Harry said.

"By the state, Raymond is in...he looks like he's out of action for a while. So, if I can get an exorcist would you come with me?" Rebecca asked.

"Yes, of course."

"Changing the subject when do you plan to go back home?"

"Next week."

"How about we spend the next couple of days just talking and relaxing?"

"Sounds good to me," Harry said, smiling.

"I need time to think about what we have just witnessed. The builder's tools in every room and discarded like they were in no hurry to come back, that is a clue. The owner said the paranormal events had started around three months ago shortly after her mother passed away. She said before that her mother lived in the house and had not experienced any weird events.

Perhaps, the owner hasn't told me everything about the history of the property and the land it sits on," Rebecca said.

"I've been thinking about what Mr Tiller said about there being a link between 'mad cow' disease and dementia. He called it the Prion. Have you heard about the Prion? I've done some research on the Internet and found some interesting information," Harry said.

"I thought we discussed that the other day," Rebecca replied.

"No, apparently the Prion is smaller than a virus and is a particle that attacks the brain of an animal or human by attaching itself to a protein that then folds out of shape. The long and short of this is you end up dying sooner than you expected because there is no cure, it's fatal in all cases. The Prion is classed as a pathogen but unlike other pathogens such as bacteria, fungi and viruses it doesn't have DNA. It's harder to kill than any living organism. I'm not saying the old man Tiller was right, but from what I've read there hasn't been a lot of research into whether a link exists or not," Harry said.

"Yes, you're right about there not being a lot of research on the matter, much like a lot of diseases that can kill you," Rebecca said.

"Yeah, this Prion is harder to kill than other pathogens, which makes it far more deadly if you happen to eat contaminated meat somewhere."

"When I saw the mass graves of the 'black death' plague in London you get a healthy respect for the little bastards that can strike you down in an instant. That's part of my job as an anthropologist studying why people died in such numbers."

Chapter 9

Later, the following week, back at CIA headquarters, Harry Steel was stood in front of his boss Michael Kurios' desk listening to the background on his next mission.

"This mission is very sensitive and requires your skillset, Harry," Michael Kurios Director of Counter Intelligence said.

Michael Kurios told Harry that a series of radar detections numbering in their tens had been received in Italy, Greece, Turkey and the latest Israel by their defence forces. He explained that the signals received showed a pattern as if they were testing those countries' defences.

"We're not sure who's behind it, we believe it's the Russians. It's your job to find out who and what is exactly going on. I can count on you to get the mission solved."

"What happening with the WHO investigation?" Harry asked.

"We've passed it over to the FBI to investigate, so it's out of our hands now," Michael replied, smiling. Continuing, he added, "We were never very good with accounting cases."

***

On the Learjet to Israel, Harry relaxed and began reading the file Michael Kurios had giving him about the mission. He had to liaise with Israel Security Service, but at the same time, the CIA liked to guard its secrets very close to its chest. Meaning they expected the other security services to share information, but it was not always the same way. That was how the CIA worked. Like a spoilt child who would not share with their siblings, he thought.

The latest radar detection was near the Sinai desert. A series of radar blips had been recorded along Israel's border with Egypt. Similar events had occurred along the borders of Italy, Greece, Turkey and Spain. There had also been witnesses to sightings of the aircraft as UFOs, which had been discounted by their respective military forces. Early intelligence suggests a Russian involvement, but so far not proven, he said to himself.

"Hi, Harry Steel, my name is Shimon Ben Daisha of Mossad, I'm here to work alongside you during this investigation," Shimon Ben Daisha said.

"Hi, yes, I'm glad you're here it saves all that fuss at customs," Harry said, smiling. Harry noticed the female agent was initially tense and failed to smile at his light-hearted words.

"We have some radar technicians and witnesses to interview. And I would like to book into my hotel and have a shower before I get going. Is that alright with you?" Harry asked.

"Yes, of course."

***

On the drive from Tel Aviv to the Israeli forward defence base at Nevatim Airbase, Harry wondered about his partner's loyalty to the CIA's way of thinking. He had been told by his boss and what was written in the file of the mission that the Russians were the chief suspects. This did not make sense to Harry as he had just spent several days working with the Russians in Mozambique and now they were being called our enemies, it did not make any sense, he said to himself.

"Can I see the recordings on the radar for that particular night?" Harry asked the radar technician.

Harry and Shimon saw the numerous blips recorded on the radar screen as the group of blips approached the perimeter of Israel's border defence.

Harry noted there were at least twenty blips approaching Israel's border with Egypt then the blips ran parallel to the coastline of Israel before just disappearing.

"Did we get a visual sighting of these blips on screen?" Harry asked.

"No, we sent up several aircraft to intercept, but no visual sightings were recorded," Shimon said. Continuing, she added, "That's why it's a mystery and I guess the reason why the CIA are interested in the matter."

"Your guess is as good as mine," Harry replied, smiling. Continuing, he added, "What about the other witnesses?"

"We have their statements."

"Yes, let me read them, but I'd like to interview them just the same," Harry said.

"Okay, I'll take you there now," Shimon said. Continuing, she added, "Do you like our country?"

"It's beautiful, but hot and sticky. And the dust gets to the back of your throat quicker than a speeding bullet," Harry remarked.

"Look! Over there a group of Bedouin on their camels are conducting their business as they have for thousands of years. From one place to another they travel across these deserts. They know where to stop for water at any time of the year. It's like mana from heaven," Shimon said.

"Hello, my name is Harry Steel and this is Shimon Ben Daisha were here to talk to you about what you saw the other night," Harry said.

"It was huge, larger than a football field and the classic shape of a flying saucer. It just hovered silently over the nuclear silos for about ten minutes and then flew away at an incredible speed and out of sight in a fraction of a second," the witness said.

"What were you doing at the time?" Harry asked.

"I was working at the olive groves around ten at night just before nightfall and as I approached my car to drive home I looked up and there in the distance I saw what I saw. I know people think I'm mad but I did see a UFO. It frightened me because the UFO was right above where the nuclear silos are situated," the witness said.

"You only saw the one UFO?" Harry asked.

"Yes, that's right, just the one."

"Could you see any identifying marks?"

"No, just lots of what looked like miniature lights from my perspective."

"What direction did the UFO fly off to?" Harry asked.

"Towards the Mediterranean Sea," the witness said.

"Have you seen any other UFOs before in the area?"

"No, this is the first time I've seen a UFO," the witness replied.

"Okay, thanks for your help," Harry said.

"What about the two airline pilots that filed a statement?" Harry asked Shimon.

"Yes, I'll contact their airline and find out when we can interview them," Shimon said.

***

On the drive towards Ben Gurion Airport on the outskirts of Tel Viv, Harry and Shimon discussed what they had found out so far surrounding the mysterious radar detection of numerous UFOs seemingly testing the Israeli border defences.

"I see from the airline pilots' statements that they saw a UFO as they were about to land at the airport. Is that unusual for pilots to report a UFO incident?" Harry asked.

"No, Israeli pilots are required to report any unusual activity in the air to the authorities," Shimon replied.

"So, other non-Israeli pilots could have witnessed a UFO at the same time and not reported it," Harry said.

"Yes, it could have happened," Shimon replied.

"I'll contact Langley and find out," Harry suggested.

Harry was soon on his mobile ringing the boffins at Langley to conduct a search for any recorded sightings of UFOs the previous week in Israeli air space. Harry wanted the proof from other airline pilots to corroborate his Israeli witnesses if he could find them.

"How long before we get to the airport," Harry asked.

"Not long now...about another hour before we get there," Shimon said.

"Do you believe what you're hearing about UFOs?" Harry asked.

"It's not my job to disbelieve or believe what is occurring. Only, to find out the truth whatever that is. I've never seen a UFO for myself, so I can't say whether another country like Russia doesn't have a hand in this," Shimon said.

"Until I see an alien it's hard to believe it's not another country like Russia or China at play," Harry said, smiling.

"You don't believe in the mass of evidence that keeps on piling up about the appearance of UFOs then?" Shimon asked.

"I've never thought too deeply about the issue until now," Harry replied. Continuing, he added, "Until I see irrefutable evidence of the existence of aliens and UFOs then I'll keep an open mind on the issue."

***

On arriving at the airport, Harry and Shimon made their way to a customs waiting room where they saw the two pilots waiting to be interviewed. They had already read the pilots statements, but Harry and Shimon were not prepared for the reaction they received from the pilots.

"Tell us what you saw that night," Harry asked.

Both pilots looked spooked as Harry tried to understand what they saw. One of the pilots looked particularly uneasy about being interviewed and was perspiring heavily in the air-conditioned room.

"Are you alright?" Harry asked.

"Yes, but we filed another sighting last night. We had another UFO fly alongside our aeroplane for several minutes before it took off at great speed and disappeared from view. It crossed in front of our aeroplane and flew around our aeroplane nearly causing us to take evasive action to avoid a collision," the pilot said.

"Was it the same type of craft you saw the other night?" Harry asked.

"Yes, the flying saucers shape around one hundred feet in diameter and a metallic-looking colour," the pilot replied.

"Let's just talk about what you saw the other night. Now, did it interfere with your flight plans that night? And what was the UFO doing?" Harry asked.

"No, it didn't interfere with our flight. The UFO was just hanging in the air...motionless...as if observing the airport from a distance," the pilot replied.

"Did you see any identifying markings on the UFO?" Shimon asked.

"None, all we could see were a series of lights around the circumference of the UFO," the pilots said.

"Have you seen anything like it before that

night?" Harry asked.

"No, not until that night," both pilots agreed.

"Now, tell us about last night's sighting."

"It looked like the same type of aircraft, but this time it tried its best to scare us into taking evasive action to avoid a collision. As we approached the airport the UFO started to dart inside and out of our flight path like it didn't care what it was doing. I'm sure some of our passengers would've seen the UFO it was that large. Easily the length of a football field...perhaps bigger," the pilot said.

"Is there anything else you can remember?" Harry asked.

"Yes, I felt like my mind was being controlled somehow and you said the same, Joe," the pilot said.

"Yeah, that's right," the other pilot agreed.

"Okay, thanks for your help," Harry and Shimon said.

***

"Where are we going now, Harry?" Shimon asked.

"To see your defence minister, I was able to get an interview arranged through Langley last night," Harry said.

"You should've asked me first...that's why I'm here as your liaison with our authorities," Shimon said annoyed at Harry's reluctance to inform her first before making arrangements to see the defence personnel.

"Sorry, it was something I did from my hotel room last night and there didn't seem the need to inform you," Harry said.

***

Harry and Shimon waited outside the office of General Gideon Simeon head of all armed services in Israel for nearly an hour before the general was ready to see them.

"Sorry, for the delay. Now, how can I help?" General Simeon asked

"Do you have any more information concerning the radar detection of numerous aircraft testing your border security?" Harry asked.

"I would like to ask why the CIA is so interested in these events." General Simeon replied. Continuing, he added, "To answer your question is none that we're willing to share."

"Look, I'm not here to hold anyone's hand, but to try and figure out what is going on and who's responsible. Now, I was told to find out the truth and report back," Harry said authoritatively.

Shrugging his shoulders, General Simeon said, "You've had access to radar data and witnesses and that's as far as Israel is willing to go. What I know is state secrets and I cannot divulge to you, Mr. Steel."

"Okay, thank you for your time," Harry said before leaving the general's office annoyed at the general's lack of cooperation.

Chapter 10

The following morning, Harry was on an aeroplane heading back to the United States looking forward to his next mission. He was still disappointed with the lack of cooperation from the Israeli defence chief. He wondered if the Israelis knew more than they were willing to share with the CIA.

At Langley, Virginia at the headquarters of the CIA, in the United States of America, Harry waited to give his boss a verbal report of his endeavours in Israel.

"Good, to see you back," Michael Kurios Director of Counter Intelligence said. Continuing, he added, "Now, tell me what you achieved in Israel?"

"Well, I don't think I achieved much, I took verbal statements from witnesses and tried to hear what the Israeli defence chief had to say, but he was unwilling to cooperate. It's all in my report, which is on your desk," Harry replied.

"Yes, I can see, but tell me what you found out, was it the Russians playing games?" Michael asked.

"A series of blips were seen by radar technicians approaching Israeli border defences. This looked like a formation of aircraft approaching their defences, but when fighter jets were deployed to get a visual identification the blips disappeared. I spoke to one witness who swears he saw a UFO about the size of a football field hover over a nearby nuclear silo site. The man said it hovered over the silos for around ten minutes before flying away at great speed. The man said the UFO was a classical saucer shape craft. I also spoke to two commercial airline pilots who reported seeing a similar UFO hovering in the vicinity of the main airport the same night as the radar blips were seen. If it was the Russians, Chinese or another country testing the Israeli defences then they have sophisticated technology that we're not aware of. That's the nuts and bolts of what I found out," Harry replied.

"Good, you've done your best. But it would've been easier if you had made a connection with the Russians or another country. It now seems we're dealing with UFOs and this is not what we're usually dealing with. Do you think we're dealing with aliens and UFOs?" Michael asked.

"No, unless I see evidence to contrary the UFOs are another country's aircraft technology," Harry replied.

"Here's the file for your mission. I want you on a flight as soon as possible. There's been a series of bombings taking place in Nebraska. So far Homeland Security and the FBI have failed to nail the culprits to the cross. We've been asked to liaise with Homeland Security and the FBI and bring the matter to a successful conclusion. Are there any questions?" Michael asked.

"Who do we think is responsible for the bombings?"

"We're not sure, but we think it's down to one of the far-right groups that seem to be popular in that region of the country. There are dozens of potential candidates, so it's your job to find out whom and put a stop to the bombings before many more people lose their lives. There's always the chance that a far-right group is being manipulated by another country like Russia. But, we're not sure," Michael said.

"What resources do I have to call on?"

"It's in the file, but the local CIA resources and of course here. Whatever it takes to find these bastards is at your disposal." Continuing, he added, "How was your holiday with your sister?"

"Great! Had time to indulge my sister with her

passion for the paranormal. Apart from that, I had time to relax and think," Harry replied.

***

On the flight to Nebraska, Harry had time to read the file his boss had given him. He noted his boss failed to mention anything about the series of cattle mutilations he was tasked to investigate as well as the series of bombings. He wondered how cattle mutilations had any connection with the bombings and wondered how his role as a CIA agent had suddenly changed in recent weeks. He had his suspicions that Michael Kurios had deliberately not told him the full truth. He could not put his finger on what that was but knew in his gut that he was not being told the truth.

He noted he was to liaise with Dr. Susan Ginsberg a thirty-five-year-old CIA asset who normally spent her time gathering information on far-right groups. Her role was to infiltrate these far-right groups and provide intelligence to the CIA so that further action could be taken if needed. She worked for the state, at the land and livestock welfare department as a microbiologist. He took a mental note of the photograph of the attractive blue-eyed blonde and committed it to memory. He wondered what type of person needs the adrenalin of working as a CIA asset when she already had a fulfilling career as a microbiologist. She sounded like a match with his sister, from the same mould and willing to take dangerous risks when they did not have to, he thought. At times, he never really understood women's behaviour as they were mysterious and beyond understanding, he said to himself. His ex-wife Angela had taught him that much as he savoured the JD and coke that he hoped would help him fall asleep on the nearly five-hour flight. He would be landing in Omaha the largest city in Nebraska.

Harry read the latest file on the bombing of the Keystone oil pipeline and wondered why Homeland Security or the FBI had not been able to find the culprits responsible, he said to himself.

***

"Hi, my name is Dr Susan Ginsberg."

"Thanks for meeting me at the airport, my name is Harry Steel. For the next few days, we're working together to help find those responsible for the recent oil pipeline bombings. I understand from your file that you work as a microbiologist for the state?" Harry said.

"Yes, that's right."

"What's this business about cattle mutilations?" Harry asked.

"Yes, we've had a spate of weird cattle mutilations over the past few weeks and many of the ranchers and farmers are annoyed with the authorities for their lack of urgency in finding out what's going on." Dr. Ginsberg replied.

"Do you know what's going on?" Harry asked.

"No, to be honest, the farmers around here have experienced cattle mutilations before but never these many occurrences. Our department has launched an enquiry, but so far they don't have any answers. So, I understand from my brief from the CIA that we are tasked to help solve the enigma," Dr. Ginsberg replied.

"Yes, heaven helps us, because it's not my usual remit. Well, let's go and see the latest cattle mutilations and start from there. We'll then speak to the local Homeland Security about the latest bombings and go from there," Harry suggested.

It was cold and windy that afternoon as Dr. Ginsberg drove Harry to the desolate ranch on the flat plains below the edge of the Rocky Mountains. Harry and Dr. Ginsberg introduced themselves to the rancher who was keen to show them his dead cattle. Harry and Dr. Ginsberg sat in the back of the rancher's jeep as he drove them to the spot on the sprawling ranch where he found the dead cattle. Harry noted that it took nearly twenty minutes to reach the dead cattle on the five thousand acre ranch from the rancher's homestead and wondered how the rancher kept track of his cattle over such distances.

When Harry and Dr. Ginsberg approached the first dead animal they could smell the disgusting odour of the decomposing animal. Harry was used to the smell of death from his early days as a Marine in the Iraqi war, but he never got used to it. The smell of death would linger in his nostrils for days, he said to himself.

"Okay, now, Mr Oakwell when did this happen or when did you find the dead cattle?" Harry asked.

"It was two days ago, early in the morning when I found the cattle. I first thought my cattle had been killed by wild animals, but then I saw no blood around each animal and how precise the injuries were. I have seen plenty of wild animal attacks on my cattle over the years, and those attacks you see rips and tears into the flesh of the cattle, but not like this. Wild animals didn't do this," the rancher insisted.

Harry noticed Dr. Ginsberg taking samples from the dead cattle as he noted how precise the wounds were on each animal. It looked to him as though someone had used some sort of sophisticated tools to remove certain parts of the cattle without leaving a cut mark. It was indeed mysterious, he said to himself.

"And there's not a footprint or tyre tracks anywhere near the cattle. The night before I found the dead cattle it rained heavily for hours. So, I don't know how they did this without leaving a trace," the rancher said.

Harry made an inspection around the site and he also found no evidence of human activity. Harry noted the depression of the earth beneath each animal, which suggested the cattle were dropped from a considerable distance in the air to their current position, which was obvious to him.

"Is this the first time you have had these kinds of attacks on your ranch?" Harry asked.

"No, I believe one other incident about five years ago. But, since then none up until these deaths," the rancher replied.

"Did you hear or see anything unusual that night," Harry asked.

"Yes, but I wasn't going to mention it, because you'll think I'm mad or something," the rancher said.

"What's that?"

"I came outside to have a smoke on the porch when I noticed strange lights in the sky...they were darting about in the distance, so they weren't stars they were UFOs," the rancher said.

"Not again," Harry remarked.

"What's that?" Dr. Ginsberg asked.

"It doesn't matter, but everywhere I go these days I hear people talking about UFOs," Harry replied.

"So, you don't believe in UFOs then?" Dr. Ginsberg asked.

"If you mean UFOs and aliens then, no I don't until I see evidence to contrary. Most UFOs are more likely to be man-made," Harry replied.

"Okay, Mr Oakwell we'll test the samples and let you know what we find, in the meantime, thanks for your help," Dr. Ginsberg said.

"Yes, thanks," Harry said.

***

On the drive towards the local Homeland

Security headquarters in Omaha to meet with special agent Dan McCuskey, Harry and Dr. Ginsberg discussed what they had seen earlier on the ranch.

"This could all be the work of some sort of black op conducted by our government and farmed out to the private sector to keep it all from the public. Whoever they are they have considerable resources to transport cattle from the ranch and conduct their work and return the dead animals back to the ranch. That much is obvious," Harry said.

"Yes, you could be right…hopefully, the samples I have will shed some light on the matter, but I don't hold out any hope on that. I have seen many cattle mutilations all over Nebraska and have taken samples before, but we are still none the wiser. In fact, there's no pattern to the occurrences that I can see," Dr. Ginsberg said.

"Why our boss and the CIA want answers to these phenomena I don't understand because it's not the normal cloak and dagger stuff I typically deal with? But, over recent months, I've become suspicious of my employers that they haven't been telling me the whole truth. I can feel it in my bones like a cold chill in winter," Harry said.

"If you're right that it's our government conducting these cattle mutilations then you have to ask what they are hoping to achieve," Dr. Ginsberg said.

"Who knows it may be what it hopes to prevent such as a disease of some type. Like foot and mouth disease. We may have to stake out a ranch and hope to catch them at it if we're lucky," Harry said.

***

Harry Steel and Dr. Ginsberg made their introductions and sat down in the office of special agent Dan McCuskey and listened to the current intelligence on the oil pipeline bombings.

"We're currently investigating two right-wing groups who we feel may be responsible for the recent oil pipeline bombings here in Nebraska. Neither has claimed responsibility, but that's normal. The American Freedom group and the Soldiers of Nebraska are the two candidates we're investigating. We've conducted raids at both camps where these groups work from and we're busy analysing what we've found," Dan McCuskey said.

"What did you find," Harry asked.

"We found some members of each group had illegal firearms, but we found no evidence of bomb-making, which was a disappointment," Dan replied.

"Can I have a copy of the file you have so far on the groups?" Harry asked.

"Yes, I have a copy already prepared for you...here it is," Dan said as he passed the file over to Harry and Dr. Ginsberg.

"What makes you think it's these two groups you have identified that may be responsible for the bombings?" Harry asked.

"Both groups have been very vocal online and in the media about their opposition to the oil pipelines. Right from the beginning, they led a campaign of disrupting the building of the pipeline," Dan said.

"Do they have a genuine reason for their opposition to the oil pipelines?" Harry asked with a soft tone of voice.

"I guess, environmental reasons and climate change," Dan replied.

"You guess that doesn't sound like you know?" Harry asked.

"Yes, I used the wrong words. They claim environmental and climate change reasons and also they say there are other pipelines that already exist that could be used for the transport of oil from the Canadian oil fields," Dan replied.

"So, they do have legitimate reasons against the construction of the new pipelines. It's a question of whether some of the members of these groups went a step more and started bombing the pipelines. Sorry, to be blunt but it also sounds to me like you have just assumptions and theories and no real evidence to speak of. It could be a lone wolf with access to the right explosives or an outside entity like a foreign country willing to conduct such actions against our country," Harry said.

"No, you're right, we don't have a shred of evidence to whom it may be," Dan said.

"I will need to visit the sites of the bombings," Harry said.

"You won't find anything because we and the FBI have been over the sites and found no clues," Dan said. Continuing, he added, "There's a map of the pipeline in the file I gave you and where the bombings occurred.

"Just the same, I need to cover all bases just in case you guys missed something," Harry said, smiling.

"I guess, that just about wraps it up for now," Dan said with an apologetic tone of voice.

"Yes, thanks for your help," Harry said.

"Yes, thanks again," Dr. Ginsberg said.

***

On the long drive up north, towards the site of the first bombing, Harry and Dr. Ginsberg discussed their meeting with Dan McCuskey. Harry and Dr. Ginsberg knew they had no hard evidence of whom it may be responsible for the pipeline bombings. Harry felt a gut instinct that it could be a lone wolf, but he was not sure, he told Dr. Ginsberg.

"So, you think it could be a lone wolf?" Dr. Ginsberg asked in a curious manner.

"At the moment, it's just a feeling nothing more. It takes a special sort of profile of the type of person to conduct such actions. There's a big difference from standing in a picket line protesting to actually making a bomb and willing to kill people," Harry replied.

"I see what you mean," Dr. Ginsberg said.

"It's pretty desolate out here on this road, we haven't seen a house or farmhouse for miles," Harry remarked.

"Yeah, you're right, but that's Nebraska miles and miles of nothing but fields of crops and the occasional car coming in the opposite direction," Dr. Ginsberg remarked, smiling.

"What's the main crop grown here in Nebraska?" Harry asked as he felt the vibration of a text message come through to his mobile. He looked at the message and saw it was his sister asking him to ring her as soon as possible.

"Soya beans."

"Concentrate on the road, while I make a call," Harry said.

"Hi, what's up?" Harry asked. His sister told him about the DNA results taken from Raymond's wounds. She explained to him that the DNA analysis could not find a match with any earthly entity known to man. She told him that she had sent the samples to another DNA laboratory for analysis to compare results and was waiting for their response.

"Okay, let me know when you have them, bye," Harry said.

"It's not far now...about an hour's drive," Dr. Ginsberg said.

"Good, I hope we can view both bomb sites in

the daylight hours, otherwise, we'll have to book into a motel for the night," Harry remarked.

When Harry and Dr. Ginsberg arrived at the first bombing site they saw the recent reconstruction of the pipeline in progress. Harry noticed how desolate the area was and how easy it would have been to plant a bomb without being seen by anyone. As they parked and got out and walked around the pipeline site they approached a construction worker.

"How long did it take to repair the pipeline since the bombing?" Harry asked.

"Around a month…since we also had to test the welds along the pipeline on either side of the bombing destruction. Luckily, there wasn't any oil flowing, otherwise, we would have had an even bigger explosion and an environmental catastrophe," the construction worker said.

"There was no one injured or killed here?" Harry asked.

"No, none that I've heard about…that happened at the latest bombing where a construction worker was working at the pumping station and was blown to pieces. That's what I heard," the construction worker replied.

"Okay, thanks for your help," Harry said.

"What do you think, Susan?"

"Well, the bomber chose a desolate place to bomb as if trying to avoid any casualty, that's for sure," Susan replied.

"Yes, I agree," Harry said with authority in his tone of voice.

"We'll have to see what the FBI have to say on the matter, perhaps they will have more information than the Homeland Security had," Susan said.

"Let's get over to the other bombing site before the light fades if we can," Harry suggested. Continuing, he added, "It's only about sixty miles down south of this location."

As Harry and Susan turned back towards the latest bombing site and they could easily see why the bomber may have chosen the locations. The area was bleak and desolate with just scrubland for miles around with no sign of any human activity. It took around an hour to reach the last bombing site, which happened to be a small pumping station, which was situated in many places along the entire length of the oil pipeline to help move the viscous oil through the pipeline they were told by the file.

"The construction worker who got killed was just doing some last-minute checks at the pumping station when the bomb went off, so it says in this file," Harry remarked.

"Yes, again another desolate place to plant a bomb not expecting anyone to be there," Susan said.

"Yes, just unfortunate for the construction worker to be in the wrong place at the time of the explosion," Harry said.

"Do you still think it was a lone wolf that carried out these bombings?" Susan asked.

"Yes, my view hasn't changed unless I see evidence to the contrary; I believe a lone wolf carried out these bombings. Perhaps, the bomber belongs to a far-right group but acted independently. Our next task is to see if the FBI has figured out where the explosives came from," Harry said.

"Tomorrow, we can check that out in Omaha," Susan remarked.

"Yeah, let's get going we have got a long drive back to the hotel and I need a drink. I've still have jet lag after the flight here," Harry suggested.

***

On the long drive back, to Omaha, Harry and Susan had time to discuss the bombing case. Harry told Susan that he felt sure his employers had not told him the full story. Harry explained that unless it was an outside entity such as a foreign country like Russia involved then normally Homeland Security and the FBI would be totally responsible for investigating the matter. Harry told Susan that something just did not sit right with his way of thinking. He did not know what it was but felt sure there was more to the case but his employers had failed to tell him.

The following morning, it was raining heavily as Susan picked up Harry at his hotel and then they drove to the local FBI headquarters to see special agent John Billows. On reaching the building they were both surprised how small the FBI headquarters were.

"Hi, my name is Harry Steel and this is Dr. Susan Ginsberg," Harry said.

"How can I help?" John Billows asked in a curious tone of voice.

"Have you found out the source of the explosives used in the two pipeline bombings?" Harry asked intently.

"Yes, it was C4 used by many construction companies in the area," Billows replied matter-of-factly.

"Is there any way of tracking who bought the explosives recently?" Harry asked intently.

"Yes, we have got a list of potential bombers who recently acquired the C4 over the past three months. We're currently cross-checking that list against known members of far-right groups to see if any links emerge. So far we've come up with zilch," Billows replied.

"It's possible the explosives were acquired in another state," Susan said.

"Yeah, you're right, that's possible and in that

case, we need to widen our net to catch our prey," Billows replied.

"Do you think it's the work of a group or a lone wolf?" Harry asked.

"My personal view is it's the work of a lone wolf and not a group of conspirators," Billows replied.

"What makes you think that?" Harry asked intently.

"Well, we've been analysing online chatter and telephone calls and have found no evidence of a group involved. This leads me to think it's the work of one person. But, its early days and anything is possible," Billows replied.

"As Susan says this lone wolf could be operating from a nearby state in the hope of covering their tracks. Could you trace all C4 purchases over the past three months from all nearby states and let me know the results?" Harry asked.

"Sorry, Harry, at the moment we don't have the jurisdiction to operate outside Nebraska. You'll have to call on the resources of the CIA to find out what you want," Billows replied.

"Okay, thanks for your help," Harry said.

"Yes, thanks," Dr. Ginsberg said.

"Sorry, I couldn't be more helpful, but at the moment, we're short-staffed due to the heightened alert level we're currently operating at," Billows said.

Harry was soon on the phone to the boys and girls in the basement of CIA headquarters in Langley, Virginia requesting assistance from Jamie a computer nerd and analyst. Harry explained to Jamie that he wanted him to run a check on all C4 purchases from three months ago and up to the present day from all nearby states bordering Nebraska.

"And where to now Harry?" Susan asked

curiously.

"Let's take another look at a nearby scene of the cattle mutilations and compare with what we saw, yesterday," Harry suggested. Continuing, he added, "Until Jamie comes up with a list of names, we're stuck in the mud as they say," Harry said.

***

After several hours of driving, they came across the ranch located in a barren landscape close to a nearby river. Harry remarked that the ranch was another desolate place and easy for any culprits to conduct their illicit activities without being disturbed. They could hear only the sound of a raven squawking on a nearby fence apart from that it was an eerily quiet landscape as they approached the rancher's home.

"Hello, Mr Sanders. My name is Harry Steel and this is Dr. Susan Ginsberg, we're here to investigate the recent cattle mutilations carried out on your ranch," Harry said.

"There's nothing to see, I cleared the dead animals away, but I took a series of photos, which you can look at," the rancher said.

"Yes, that's fine," Harry said.

"When did you find the cattle mutilations?" Susan asked.

"It was over a week ago, now. I found six of my cattle dead with a number of injuries. Some of the animals had what looked like precision cuts to their bodies. Some had their eyes removed and others had their rear ends removed, but no blood was found around the animals. It wasn't the work of wild animals because I've seen plenty of attacks on my cattle over the years and they just leave a bloody mess," the rancher said with a worried tone of voice.

"Did you hear or see anything that night?" Susan

asked intently.

"Yes, strange lights moving fast around the ranch early that morning around four in the morning, not yet day. I've seen strange lights in the sky over the years and paid no attention to them. But, it must have frightened the cattle because they were making lots of noise, which isn't normal…usually at night they are quiet," the rancher replied.

"Can we have a look at the photos you took?" Harry asked.

The rancher showed Harry and Susan the photos of the cattle mutilations and they were not shocked at what they saw they had seen similar the day before. The rancher gave Harry and Susan a couple of the photos to keep for reference.

"Could you take us to where you found the dead cattle?" Harry asked.

"Yeah, climb into my land rover and I'll take you there," the rancher said.

After about twenty minutes they arrived at the scene of the previous week's cattle mutilations. Harry and Susan saw several areas where the land was depressed by a great force. They also noticed how desolate the area was.

"It's very similar to yesterday's experience where some of the ground is depressed under where the animal was found," Susan said.

"Yeah, I've noticed the same. Did you notice the land was depressed when you found the dead cattle?" Harry asked.

Shrugging his shoulders, the rancher replied, "Yes, under each animal the land had been crushed as though the animal had been dropped from a great distance from high up in the air."

Harry walked around the scene to look for any

clues but found none. He could only see the impressions in the ground where the cattle were found dead.

"Okay, Mr Sanders we've seen enough for now," Harry said.

"Do you know who is responsible for my dead cattle?" the rancher asked as he drove Harry and Susan back to the homestead.

"At the moment, no, but we're on the case and will let you know when we have more information," Harry replied with a calm tone of voice.

**

On the drive back to Omaha, Harry and Susan discussed what they had seen and compared notes. Susan told Harry that she had previously taken samples from the dead animals, but the results failed to deliver any conclusions. Other than sophisticated tools must have been used to remove the organs and flesh at what she had seen.

"I even had a surgeon look at the cattle wounds and he said he would struggle to make such injuries without the need for some sort of laser to precisely cut away flesh and remove organs," Susan remarked.

"So what is your assumption?" Harry asked.

"I hate to commit myself, but I don't think it's our government or another organisation. Like most of the ranchers and farmers around here, I think it's down to an unknown source. If that is UFOs and aliens then it wouldn't surprise me," Susan replied.

"Not you as well, the last few weeks I've heard nothing but UFOs and aliens," Harry remarked, laughing.

"You don't believe its aliens then?" Susan asked.

"No, not until I see verifiable proof then I'll change my mind," Harry said.

"So what's your assumption?" Susan asked.

"I just don't know and I don't like to make assumptions because I was taught that making assumptions can cost lives," Harry replied. Continuing, he added, "If I was betting man and I'm not, but if I was then I would put money on it being a government-sponsored operation."

"Well, it's costing the ranchers and farmers who experience these attacks on their animals a considerable amount of money. You'd have thought the government would conduct their operations on a secluded farm or ranch somewhere in secret without needing to steal the livestock," Susan said.

"It could be a rogue outfit who have been given carte blanche to do what they want. So, unless we catch these bastards at it, we stand very little chance of catching them. They must have considerable resources like helicopters to lift and transport the cattle to where they conduct their illicit operations," Harry insisted. Continuing, he added, "What I don't understand is why we have seen no reports of helicopters with cattle hanging from them in the area. Someone surely would have seen something even late at night."

"Yes, you're right. I've seen no reports of such activity, which like you say is strange, to say the least. I've read about cattle mutilations in other states and have seen no reports of helicopters being seen," Susan said.

"Let's get back to your place of work so we can use your computers," Harry suggested.

***

At Susan's place of work, they waited for Jamie at the CIA headquarters to send an email to Susan's computer so they could print out a list of potential bombers and last known addresses.

"Hi, Jamie, run the list against suspects with criminal form and then send me what you have," Harry

said.

"I'm sending an email, now," Jamie said.

"It looks like we've our work cut out. We've got eight names and addresses to check out in all the bordering states to Nebraska," Harry said. Continuing, he added, "Jamie, run the last eight names against any ties with far-right groups and forward what comes up."

"Okay, will do," Jamie replied.

"I thought you said it was a lone wolf responsible for the bombings?" Susan queried.

"Yes, I still think the same, but the person may belong to a far-right group and is acting independent of them," Harry replied thoughtfully.

"Hi, Harry, sending an email now," Jamie said.

"That's better we've only three people to check out now," Harry said. Continuing, he added, "We have only three states to visit, Iowa, Colorado and Wyoming that have corresponding purchases with ties to far-right groups.

"Where to start first," Susan said.

"I suggest we start up northwest and the closest state to the bombings and that would be Wyoming," Harry suggested.

"From here its best if we catch a flight to Cheyenne it will take less time to get there. And the suspect lives close to the capital," Susan suggested.

"Yes, I agree."

***

Before they boarded the aeroplane for the two-hour flight to Cheyenne, Wyoming they had Jamie at CIA headquarters run a detailed profile of a Joseph Zyleic from the day he was born to the present day. As Harry and Susan sat in business class they studied the profile of the suspect.

Joseph Zyleic was born in Czechoslovakia and

was brought to America with his parents and now was an American citizen. For most of his life, he had worked in the construction industry. And he had only recently retired two years ago. He was divorced and had two grown-up children, but lived alone. He was a member of the Nebraska Freedom Fighters a far-right group, but the group was not known for any anti-social behaviour. He had three criminal convictions, two convictions for bar-room fights and one conviction for armed robbery of a liquor store, which all happened when he was in his early twenties, but since then he had a clean slate.

"What do you think, Susan?" Harry asked.

"Seems pretty ordinary to me, except for his criminal past, which happened in his youthful days," Susan replied.

Harry shrugged his shoulders and said, "Yes, I agree, but it's nearly always the quiet ones you have to watch for." Continuing, he added, "A bit like me."

"Perhaps, something major happened in his life and he changed," Susan said, smiling.

"Hold on, we're getting ahead of ourselves, perhaps this man is innocent and we're condemning him before we know the facts," Harry said.

***

On landing at Cheyenne, Harry and Susan hired a vehicle and were soon on their way to see Mr Joseph Zyleic with the aid of a Satnav to guide them there. Just in case, Harry told Susan to check her gun and make sure it was loaded and the safety off. As Harry and Susan approached the home of Joseph Zyleic they saw the bungalow was in need of repair and the gardens surrounding the property were overgrown with weeds. The property was in a quiet street in the suburbs of the city around ten miles from the centre of Cheyenne. They parked on the street and made their way to the front door and knocked.

"Hi, we're here to talk to Mr Joseph Zyleic," Harry said.

"That's me, who are you?" the old man asked.

"My name is Harry Steel and this is Dr Susan Ginsberg, we both work for the CIA. Can we come in...we would like to ask you some questions," Harry replied.

Harry's first impression of the old man was that he looked frail and looked as though walking a few yards would be a stretch for the old man, he thought.

"You've heard about the oil pipeline bombings in Nebraska have you any involvement in that?" Harry asked.

"Are you joking, can't you see how I struggle to get about these days. Besides, I wouldn't commit such a crime it's beyond me," the old man replied.

"Have you any idea whom may be behind such a crime?" Susan asked.

"No, the men and women I met in the Nebraska Freedom Fighters were solid people, not prone to committing crimes. That was fifteen years ago when I would spend the weekend's playing soldiers. Since then, I've had no contact with anyone from the group. Since the back problems, I've kept to myself much of the time," the old man said.

"Right, I understand, but you purchased some C4 around a month ago, how do you explain that?" Harry asked.

"Simple, I bought some for a friend and used it to blow up a derelict property for him, which was cheaper than using a conventional crane and ball to demolish the property. The ground has been cleared of all the mess, but you can speak to the owner if you wish. The ground is about forty miles from here and you need to speak to Jeff Anders about this," the old man said.

"So, you can get around when you have to," Harry said.

Grimacing in his chair, the old man said, "Yes, I've my good and bad days with my back problems, but mostly bad. Here's Jeff's address and mobile number."

"Thanks, we'll check it out and thanks for your time," Harry said.

Back in their vehicle they rang the mobile number for Jeff Anders and arranged a meeting with him later that day.

"What did you think of Mr Joseph Zyleic?" Harry asked curiously.

"He's either a very good actor and a liar or a genuine old man not capable of such crimes," Susan replied, nonchalantly. Continuing, she added, "What about you?"

"I'm not too sure, especially after his reply to the last question. His reply seemed too convenient and rehearsed as if he was expecting it. Like you say; either a very good actor and a liar or a genuine innocent person. I'll make up my mind when we have seen Mr Jeff Anders and see what he has to say," Harry replied.

As they travelled along the deserted road to the home of Mr Jeff Anders, Harry told Susan how much he hated flying even though he had to fly to most of his missions. He told Susan that as an eight-year-old boy he experienced the aeroplane that he was on nearly crash on arrival. This was the reason he hated flying.

"Flying is so unnatural when you consider we're travelling around the sun at around seventeen thousand miles per hour," Harry said nonchalantly.

"So, it's a genuine fear of flying?" Susan asked curiously.

"Yes and no is the answer. Yes, it's a fear but no

I don't fear death. If fate decides my time is up then there's not much I can do about it. From what I've read the cosmos isn't in chaos. Scientists have found patterns in the cosmos. Hard to see at first but they are there to see. So, that must mean the cosmos is deterministic in nature meaning that an unseen force, call it fate, plays a role in our lives, like it or not," Harry said philosophically.

"So, you believe in fate?" Susan asked curiously.

"Yes, it happens whether we like it or not. It's often the smallest detail that nails a criminal to the cross. If you analyse deeply enough you'll find fate played its hands in the matter. Take the case we're on now, before this case I would've never met you. In a way, that's fate bringing two people together who would've not met otherwise," Harry said, smiling.

"Yes, but that happens all the time in people's lives," Susan said gleefully.

"Yeah, you're right, but some of those encounters mean something in the long run. Have you heard about quantum entanglement? It goes something like this; in the sub-atomic world of particles of atoms, they call the quantum realm. Essentially, if you have a particle divided and separated by millions and millions of miles they can react to each other even though they're separated by vast distances. This seemingly goes against our understanding of the world and what our brains will accept. But, it's true; scientists have conducted experiments and proved the theory of quantum entanglement. This is strange but true," Harry said.

"Sounds weird, but you say true?" Susan asked incredulously.

"Yes, scientists have proved the existence of quantum entanglement."

"How does that prove that fate plays a hand in

our lives?" Susan asked intently.

"It seemingly proves that an unseen force can have an effect on something over vast distances, so the chances are that fate works in the same way," Harry replied nonchalantly.

"So, what do you think about this case," Susan said intently.

"Something just doesn't sit right for me. But, I wouldn't be surprised if it was the smallest detail that hammers in the nail," Harry said confidently.

Susan shrugged her shoulders and said, "You may be right."

"It's not conventional to use C4 to blow up a property! Don't you just spread the mess everywhere and then you spend more time cleaning up? That just doesn't sit right with me as a reason. Like I said before, too convenient an answer," Harry said positively.

***

"Hello, Mr Anders, my name is Harry Steel and this is Dr. Susan Ginsberg."

"I understand from Mr Joseph Zyleic that he was employed by you to blow up a property using C4 explosives, is that correct?" Harry asked.

"Yes, that's right...an old brick-built building that was ripe for demolition," Jeff Anders said.

"Isn't that unconventional to use C4 explosives to demolish the building?" Harry asked.

"Yes, but Mr Zyleic placed the explosives in such a way the building collapsed in on itself without the need for a crane and ball demolition, thereby, saving many hours with a crane and ball on hire. Can I ask what's this all about...I have all the building and demolition tickets if you would like to see them?" Mr Anders replied.

"Yes, show me."

"Here are the building and demolition tickets."

"Right, thanks, we may have to keep these until further notice, is that alright?" Harry asked.

"Yes, that's okay."

"Can you show us the site of the demolition?" Harry asked.

"Yeah, follow me in your vehicle, but there's not much to see," Mr Anders said.

After a short drive to the site, Harry and Susan inspected the area, which was now a hive of activity with builders now in the process of building another property. Harry spoke to one of the builders about the site and was satisfied with what he was told as Mr Anders looked on from his car.

"You knew the property before it was demolished?" Harry asked.

"Yeah, it was a brick-built building," the building worker said.

"It was a former slaughterhouse," another worker said.

"Oh, what are you building, now?" Harry asked.

"Three houses on this site," the building worker said.

"Okay Mr Anders you can go, we'll make our own way back, thanks," Harry said.

"Can I ask what this is all about?" Mr Anders asked again.

"Yes, the Nebraska oil pipeline bombings, you wouldn't know anything about that would you?" Harry asked intently.

"Ummm, no I wouldn't know anything about that," Mr Anders replied.

"Are you sure?"

"Yeah, I'm sure," Mr Anders replied briskly and annoyed at being asked such a question.

"Good, because it's now murder the bomber is wanted for," Harry said.

On the way back to Omaha, Harry and Susan discussed what they thought about their first suspect and compared notes. They were both undecided on whether the suspect was guilty or not. But, they were eager to see their next suspect in South Dakota. It was only a short flight to Sioux Falls the largest city in the state. From there it would only be a relatively short drive to their next suspect's home address in Mitchell.

The suspect was Mr Arthur Turnball a retired civil engineer who recently bought a quantity of C4 for an unspecified reason. In his youth, he had committed an assault on a person in a bar and was duly charged and was given probation, but since then had been a law-abiding citizen.

As Harry and Susan approached the house in a leafy tree-lined neighbourhood of tidy gardens and streets they knocked on the front door and were greeted by an old man in a wheelchair.

"Hello, Mr Turnball my name is Harry Steel and this Dr. Susan Ginsberg we're here to ask you a few questions about your recent purchase of C4, is that alright?" Harry asked.

"Yeah, go ahead."

"What did you buy the C4 for?" Harry asked intently.

"To blow this place up with me in it, I wanted to kill myself," the old man said.

"So, you haven't used the C4 yet, is that right?" Susan asked.

"Yeah, that's right, it's in the garage safe and sound until I decide to use it," the old man said.

"Isn't dangerous to have C4 stored in the garage?" Harry asked.

"No, it's perfectly safe without the donators attached," the old man said. Continuing, he added, "Without an electrical charge to the donators the C4 is harmless as is the donators without an electrical current applied to them."

"Can we see the C4 in the garage and your purchase ticket?" Susan asked.

"Yes, here you are and the C4 is on the garage bench you can't miss it!" the old man said.

"I didn't realise it was so easy to acquire high explosives," Harry said to Susan as they saw the C4 on the bench as the old man had said. Harry noted that the quantity of C4 matched the purchased ticket and he was satisfied the old man was telling the truth.

"Oh, just one more question. Would you use C4 to blow up a brick built building rather than use a crane and ball to demolish the building?" Harry asked.

"No, not for me because you need too many permits and that will take time. And in the time it takes to get a permit you could've demolished the building without the need for explosives," the old man said.

Harry and Susan thanked Mr Turnball for his time and decided to catch the next flight back to Omaha. They had one more suspect to visit and that would be for the following day.

Chapter 11

The following morning, Harry and Susan decided to drive to their next suspect's home in Sioux City, Iowa. It's was raining heavily, and the wind was gusting along the highway with the mighty Missouri River on their left-hand side.

The suspect's home was a houseboat with a storage shack and yard, which the owner a Mr. Singh Ibrahim a thirty-five-year-old, ex-Marine who had served in the last Gulf War with distinction was currently living at. His current occupation was listed as a welder. The houseboat was ready and waiting for the owner to cast off for a trip down the mighty Missouri River. Harry and Susan realised the houseboat had sailed only hours before their arrival they were told by another houseboat neighbour.

"What's the boat called?" Harry asked.

"It's called the Lake Jelly!" the neighbour said.

"What type of boat is it?" Harry asked intently.

"It's a former barge with a single mast for a sail like a sloop," the neighbour replied.

"Okay, thanks for your help."

"Susan, we need to find a boat and follow them down the Missouri River," Harry suggested.

"I'll take you in my boat!" the neighbour said.

"Great, cast off as soon as possible!" Harry suggested.

"My name is Eric," the neighbour said to Harry and Susan.

"Why didn't you call in the river police?" Susan asked.

"Because the suspect is not under arrest and we may inadvertently alarm our suspect," Harry replied nonchalantly.

"People sail up and down the river all the time," Eric said to Harry and Susan.

The river looked cold and uninviting as Harry and Susan scanned the river ahead looking for any boat that fitted the description of the suspect's Lake Jelly boat. The suspect was several hours ahead, but Harry hoped to catch up at some point and board the boat. They watched as a flock of geese flew overhead and landed on a barren part of the shoreline, and the geese immediately started squawking and announcing their presence to all in the vicinity. It was not long before the daylight faded into the shadows of the moonlight and Eric switched on his boat lights for the night as Harry and Susan went below to the galley leaving Eric to steer the boat and keep a lookout for the Lake Jelly.

"Isn't unusual for us to be chasing our suspect when we could've waited for him to return?" Susan asked nonchalantly.

"Yes, but he could've been away for some time and we can't wait to find the bomber before another bombing happens," Harry replied.

"Do you think it could be the bomber?" Susan asked intently.

"I don't think unless I have some facts, we'll have to see what the suspect has to say on the matter," Harry replied authoritatively. Continuing, he added, "I have my doubts about the first suspect's story, the old man in the wheelchair."

"Yes, some of his stories just don't fit right like you said," Susan said with an authoritative tone of voice.

"But, I feel we're getting closer to solving this case the more I think about it. We have got the task of interviewing our next suspect and to see what he has to say about the matter," Harry said.

Suddenly, they heard the sound of a horn

blowing as another boat passed by in the darkness. Harry and Susan looked through the portholes and saw only the lights of the passing boat as Eric carefully steered the boat down the river by the light of the full moon. Normally, most pleasure boats would lay anchor for the night before continuing their journey in the daylight hours, Eric told Harry and Susan. Luckily, Eric could avoid any obstacles in the river like fallen trees by the moonlight, which provided enough light to see any dangers well ahead of time.

"What's the background on our suspect Mr Singh Ibrahim?" Susan asked.

"It seems he did a year inside for a fraud conviction with a year's probation. That was early in his life and then he joined the Marines, which is no mean feat. As you know, I was in the Marines. That should've straightened him out, but we shall see," Harry replied.

"No convictions since sounds like it did sort him out," Susan said nonchalantly.

"Going off the subject, what made you want to join the CIA?" Harry asked intently.

"As a microbiologist, I miss the adrenalin rush of solving cases for the CIA. Working for the local state government as a microbiologist just doesn't cut it for me. I joined to help protect the people. But, since the breakout of a rash of cattle mutilations it has stimulated my interest in my job as now the CIA want to know what's going on, just as much as me," Susan replied.

"And what do you think is going on?" Harry asked intensely.

"You mean the cattle mutilations?" Susan asked.

"Yes, of course."

"I'm not sure; like you said unless we catch the bastards at it then we have little chance of solving the case. Unless it's really is an alien fucking with our food supply. Did you know that cattle share much of their DNA with humans?" Susan replied, smiling. Continuing, she added, "It could be that we're the experiment, but we're not aware of it, yet!"

"How's that work?"

"Well, first forget about all you have heard about genes and understand that our DNA contains a blueprint to make a human, but we also share much of the same DNA with cattle. Now, when a cell grows it uses its DNA profile to make whatever that cell is asked to produce such as brain cells or muscle cells. Certain parts of the DNA sequence are switched on or off and parts are then used to form whatever cell to produce. These are the parts of the DNA that are referred to as genes, but strictly speaking there is no such thing as a gene. It's just a word to describe a series of proteins that act together to produce something. If someone wanted to fuck with our food supply and experiment on us at the same time then they're going about it the right way. They didn't before with 'mad cow' disease," Susan said intently.

"Do you think we're an experiment?" Harry asked nonchalantly.

"Think about the exponential growth of dementia in society. You have to ask why that suddenly appeared in the last twenty to thirty years or so," Susan replied.

"What was that you said about 'mad cow' disease?" Harry asked.

"Well, back in the eighties some fools thought that…it was a good idea to feed herbivores meat, which caused 'mad cow' disease in cattle and in humans Creutzfeldt-Jakob disease, which is fatal in all cases. The experiment was when the government said it was safe to eat the meat…when it clearly wasn't. People died within a year of showing symptoms of the disease," Susan said.

"Why did some people catch the disease and

others didn't?" Harry asked intently.

"It depended on whether you had eaten an affected part of the meat, such as the nerve cord and other tissues of the animal. But, also they mentioned the Prion, which turns out to be one hard nut," Susan said.

"What's that about the Prion?" Harry asked in a curious tone of voice.

"It's smaller than a virus and harder to kill. Even extreme temperatures have a difficult time killing the little bastards. The governments at the time said they may manifest themselves in twenty to thirty years' time that would be around two thousand and sixteen, now, at the same time dementia took off like an aeroplane into our lives. It's only a theory. Not much research has been done into dementia and other related diseases and the possible links to the Prion," Susan said.

Suddenly, Harry and Susan heard a loud thud and felt the boat shudder like it had hit something hard.

"What was that?" Harry shouted out to Eric.

"Sorry, we caught the tail end of a large tree. No damage though," Eric shouted back.

"It's best if you try and get some sleep. I'll keep watch with Eric and wake you in a few hours," Harry said.

"Okay, will do."

Harry went up top with Eric to see if he needed a rest. It was still night and it would be several hours before dawn.

"Do you need a rest, Eric?" Harry asked.

"No, I'm fine, I just need a coffee to keep me going," Eric suggested.

"No worries, milk and sugar?" Harry asked.

"Yes, it's all in the fridge in the galley," Eric said.

"Here, you are one coffee," Harry said.

"What can you tell me about your neighbour?" Harry asked intently.

"Not much, he says hello, but doesn't spend time talking to me. He sometimes has a woman staying with him, but apart from that, he keeps to himself. Is he in big trouble with the law?" Eric asked intently.

"That's what we need to find out apart from that I can't say anymore," Harry replied. Continuing, he added, "Do you spend much time on your boat?"

"Yes, as much as I can. I've got a house in Sioux City, but since I retired I try and spend much of it going up and down the river. I find it very relaxing past time," Eric remarked.

"Perhaps, I will buy a boat when I retire and do the same," Harry remarked.

"Morning, Harry…Eric," Susan said.

"I'll get some sleep if I can…call me if you see the suspect's boat," Harry said to Eric and Susan.

Harry tried to make the cabin bed comfortable and gradually he fell asleep to the relaxing sound of the hull skimming through the water. His mind had drifted off as he thought about what Susan had said about the Prion. He remembered, his sister had mentioned the same entity and wondered if they were both right about the Prion. Harry knew governments often played devil's advocate with people's lives, he said to himself.

***

"Wake up, Harry…we've spotted the boat!" Susan said franticly.

"It's up ahead…moored by that wooden jetty on the right," Eric said as he passed the binoculars to Harry.

"Are you sure…I can't see its name?" Harry asked incredulously.

"Yes, that's the Lake Jelly boat, for sure."

"Okay, pull up beside the boat…and I'll call

out."

"Hello, Mr Ibrahim...Hello Mr Ibrahim," Harry shouted out.

"Hello...hello..."

Harry noticed the man had just woken up and was unprepared for visitors. Harry flashed his CIA identity card and introduced himself and Dr. Susan Ginsberg to the suspect.

"May we come aboard we need to ask you a few questions?" Harry asked as he made his way aboard the boat.

"Yes, what's this all about?" Mr Ibrahim asked.

"It's about that C4 you bought the other day," Harry said. Continuing, he added, "Why did you buy it?"

"I've still got it...I haven't used it, yet. I bought it for a construction job, I plan to do in a few weeks' time," Mr Ibrahim replied.

"And what would that be?" Harry pressed for an answer.

"Oh, removal of granite stone for a customer with a garden project in Sioux City," Mr Ibrahim replied. Continuing, he added, "Here are the customer's details."

"Thanks, we'll check it out," Harry said. Continuing, he added, "Where's the C4 being stored?"

"At my shack near my mooring back close to Sioux City," Mr Ibrahim replied. Continuing, he added, "It's safe as houses without the detonators. What's this all about, anyway?"

"The oil pipeline bombings in Nebraska," Harry retorted.

"I don't know anything about that," Mr Ibrahim said firmly.

"What about your companion?" Harry asked.

"How did you know...?"

"I could smell the coffee being made," Harry

replied, smiling.

"Sonia can you make some coffee for our two guests," Mr Ibrahim shouted down below deck. Continuing he added, "This is my girlfriend Sonia Hermes."

"Do you know anything about the Nebraska oil pipeline bombings?" Harry asked.

"No, didn't even know there had been a bombing," Sonia replied.

"Okay, thanks for your help, we'll be on our way," Harry said. Continuing, he added, "Oh, just one more question. Is that usual to use C4 to blast granite?"

"Yes and no, C4 does the job and its cheap and safe. You could use another explosive such as dynamite, but it's not safe to use," Mr Ibrahim replied.

Harry and Susan said thanks again and made their way back to Eric's boat for their return journey close to Sioux City. Harry was soon on his mobile speaking to Jamie at CIA headquarters in Langley, Virginia.

"Let's get going, Eric," Harry demanded. Continuing, he added, "We've no time to waste."

"Hi Jamie, I need you to run a check on all calls made by Mr Ibrahim in the last three months up to and including the present day. Let me have the information as soon as possible," Harry asked.

"You suspect something?" Susan asked.

"Yes, just filling in the blanks. We also need to check his story with this customer in Sioux City," Harry suggested.

***

"Hi, my name is Harry Steel and this is Dr. Susan Ginsberg; we're here to ask you a few questions about your garden project. We understand from Mr Ibrahim that he's employed by you to blast some granite. Is that correct?" Harry asked.

"Yes, that's correct. I need some large boulders for a garden project and he said he could do it for me. Is there a problem?" the client asked.

"No problem, we're just checking when people buy high explosives," Harry replied. Continuing, he added, "You heard about the oil pipeline bombings in Nebraska?"

"No, I must have missed that," the client replied.

"Where do you plan to get your granite from?" Susan asked.

"There's an abandoned quarry not far from here…around a twenty minutes" drive," the client replied. Continuing, she added, "Near a town called Freemont."

"What's the name of the quarry?" Susan asked intently.

"The Freemont Quarry," the client replied.

"Okay, thanks for your help," Harry and Susan said together.

"Oh, just one more question. How did you meet Mr Ibrahim?" Harry asked intently.

"I placed a wanted ad online with the problem and he phoned with a solution?" the client replied.

"Where was that ad placed?"

"On the local Craig's list platform," the client replied.

"Okay, thanks again for your help," Harry said.

***

On the drive back to Omaha, Harry received a call from his sister.

"Hi, what's up?"

"I've just received the DNA results from the second laboratory this afternoon. The results correspond with the first laboratory…there a match to an alien species. The DNA is not from this planet. What do you think about that?" Rebecca asked cheerfully.

"Are you sure?" Harry asked incredulously.

"Well, both of the laboratories are world leaders in DNA analysis...so I see no reason to doubt the results," Rebecca replied confidently.

"Look, I can't talk right now, speak to you later," Harry said as he hung up the call.

"Is everything all right?" Susan asked intently.

"Yes, keep your eyes on the road! It was just some unfinished business," Harry replied sharply. He did not want to reveal his private life to a work colleague, especially the subject of the possibility of the existence of aliens. Besides, he felt sure there was a logical explanation to his sister's DNA evidence, he said to himself.

"Okay, boss!"

"I didn't mean to be blunt, but the traffic on this road is getting heavy. It must be that time of day when everyone tries to make a mad dash to get home after a day's work."

"What did you think about Mrs Gina Spinlotti the customer who employed Ibrahim to blow up some granite?" Susan said.

"Seems genuine, but I'm not sure," Harry replied intently.

"Why?"

"It's just a hunch! There are several candidates at the moment and I'll let you know more tomorrow," Harry replied, smiling. Continuing, he added, "What are your thoughts on Mrs Gina Spinlotti?"

"She seems genuine enough, but it's strange to place an ad in the wanted pages when you can just call a quarry and find the granite that way," Susan said as she pulled off the highway onto the slip road that led to the

Freemont Quarry.

The light was starting to fade as they pulled up outside the abandoned quarry. They both noticed the abandoned plant machinery already rusting away and no sign of anyone keeping a watch on the quarry.

"Don't you think it's weird that you can just walk right in here and do what the hell you like?" Harry said.

"Yeah, it doesn't add up...surely there're health and safety issues to apply to? Someone will be responsible, that's for sure," Susan replied.

"And it's been bugging me since our meeting with Mr Ibrahim."

"What's that, Harry?"

"Well, you'd need a heavy lifting plant and a truck to transport the granite boulders and depending on the weight...that could add up to some serious equipment. And our Mr Ibrahim doesn't have that sort of equipment to deal with such a project. And like you said before...why wouldn't you just make a call to a quarry...that have all the necessary equipment and have them deliver the goods. We need to make a visit to Mr Ibrahim's shack and see if the C4 is stored there as he said, but I've got a feeling it won't be and we've found the bomber," Harry said grimly.

"Do you think Spinlotti is in on it?"

"Not sure, but we'll soon find out," Harry replied.

"Don't we need a warrant for such action?" Susan asked pensively.

"We don't have time for that...our mission is to stop the bomber. The local and federal authorities can pick up the pieces, we just need to stop another bomb exploding before more people get injured or killed," Harry replied.

***

On the short drive to Ibrahim's shack, Harry made a call to CIA headquarters to speak to Jamie in the basement. Harry wanted information on Mrs. Spinlotti.

"Hi, Jamie can you get me all information on Mrs Gina Spinlotti," Harry said as he gave Jamie her address details. He had a hunch like an itch you had to scratch.

"You think she's involved?" Susan asked intently.

"We'll soon find out."

When Harry and Susan arrived at the road leading to Ibrahim's shack by the Missouri River they heard a loud explosion. They noticed the police vehicle by the roadside covered with debris from the explosion and assumed the worst. They saw a police officer frantically looking for something among the destruction, but it was a forlorn endeavour. Harry immediately thought the bomb was laid for him and Susan if they had made the mistake of trying to enter the shack.

"What happened?" Harry asked.

"My partner and I got a call to attend a possible break-in, when my partner tried to enter the whole place blew up. It was a trap!" the police officer said.

"Yes, you're right and the person responsible wanted someone to trigger the bomb to conceal the evidence. That's two murders to account for and it's possible another bomb set to go off somewhere else," Harry said grimly. Continuing, he added, "Susan, I want this river searched from here down as far as it goes by the river police and by helicopter for the Lake Jelly boat. Have the helicopter pick us up here and we'll begin our search for the bastards!"

Within minutes, Harry and Susan were inside the helicopter travelling down the Missouri River looking for the Lake Jelly boat. They also had the river police searching every inlet and boat on the river.

Over the noise of the helicopter blades, Susan asked, "Do you think we'll find them on the river?"

"No, we have to start somewhere and besides he may have failed to leave us a clean slate. It's often the smallest detail that criminals leave behind that nails them to the cross," Harry said nonchalantly.

**

After an exhaustive search, the Lake Jelly boat was spotted by a local police officer who was searching jetties and docks along the western side of the Missouri River working in a southerly direction. According to local witnesses, the boat had been docked for at least close to twenty-four hours before the police officer found it. None of the witnesses had seen the occupants of the boat leave the area. Harry and Susan assumed that the suspects had made their escape during the night or early morning.

Harry carefully approached the boat after he previously had the bomb squad of the local police force check for any explosives that may have been placed to kill more people. Susan watched every move Harry was making before Harry beckoned Susan forward to make an inspection below the deck of the boat. Harry and Susan noticed how well stocked with food the galley cupboards were and could easily see how two people could live aboard the boat if they wanted to. The galley held a microwave, fridge, hob cooker and tea and coffee making pots. They saw a small TV in the corner of the cabin and space for four fold-down beds. It looked like the couple was planning a leisure trip down the river until Harry and Susan had scuppered the couple's plans.

"It looks like they took off when they knew we were on their tail," Harry said.

"Yeah, we spoilt their plans, unless they planned to leave at these docks and had a vehicle ready and waiting," Susan said.

"I prefer they had someone pick them up from here," Harry said. Continuing, he added, "People don't spend money on stocking up with food without a plan. We changed their plans. So, now, we have the suspects on the run."

"What's your plan now?" Susan asked intently.

"Keep looking, we may find something and then we take the chopper back to your car and drive back to Omaha and continue the search tomorrow," Harry replied.

***

On the way back to pick up Susan's vehicle, Harry was on the phone with the local police force and requesting to view any CCTV coverage of the main highway between where the Lake Jelly boat was moored and Ibrahim's exploded shack by the river.

Inside the local police headquarters, Harry and Susan were busy viewing the CCTV recordings of the previous night's footage. When Harry spotted the make and license plates of Miss Gina Spinlotti's vehicle heading south along the highway at three fifteen in the morning. They noticed that there was a gap of around one hour and seventeen minutes before another camera along the highway picked up the car again. Harry figured there was plenty of time to drive onto the slip road and make it to where the boat was moored and back again onto the highway. Harry found out that the cameras were placed at certain spots and not at all the same distance apart.

As Harry and Susan continued to watch the CCTV footage and they soon realised that their suspects had disappeared or stopped somewhere. Harry and Susan felt sure the bombers next target would be somewhere in Nebraska.

"What makes you think their next target will be in Nebraska?" the police captain asked.

"Because I'm following their MO... their first two bombings were in Nebraska, so it follows their next is likely to be in Nebraska as well," Harry replied.

"I copy that," Susan muttered.

"They're on the run, so we've upset their plans, but I still believe they'll try and hit their original target and get away," Harry said.

"I've got an all car lookout for the vehicle and the suspects...sooner or later we'll find them," the police captain said.

"Hopefully, before another bomb goes off," Susan remarked.

"Yeah, copy that," the police captain muttered. Continuing, he added, "What do you think will be their next target?"

"Not sure...same MO again...then it's likely to be something to do with the Keystone oil pipeline. It all depends on what's going through this madman's mind. What's the difference between a pacifist and a terrorist's mind is probably a whole load of psychobabble and not much else. I normally find the commonest reasons why some people kill people are sex or money. Or at least, that's the initial attraction to being evil or greedy," Harry replied thoughtfully.

"Sounds like you have this perp's MO down to the ground," the police captain muttered.

"It could be a whole lot of reasons why this perp is doing what they're doing, besides sex and money. Perhaps, there's a grudge against the Keystone oil pipeline, because of this or that. How many turn-offs are there between the last two cameras?" Susan asked.

"Just one on either side," the police captain replied.

"My guess is they took the right-hand turnoff and disappeared along that road. What's along that road before another camera?" Harry asked intently.

"A series of farms and ranches and a small town called Aurora. There's not another camera until you reach the junction of two main roads and the oil pipeline junction where several pipelines naturally converge. The convergence of these oil pipelines into one terminal where the oil is again pumped or transferred to train containers and transported to several different parts of America. The terminal was built outside the town for safety and environmental reasons," the police captain replied. Continuing, he added, "You don't think the terminal could be the targets do you?"

"Yes, it's plausible the bomber wants to make a statement and bombing the terminal would make a statement and an ecological catastrophe at the same time. I would get some extra security out there just in case," Harry said intently.

"You think it's a possible target, Harry?" Susan asked with disbelief in the tone of her voice.

"Yes, I believe it's been their aim from the beginning. We disturbed their plans and just maybe forced their hand," Harry replied meaningfully.

"What do you mean by that?" the police captain asked curiously.

"They probably had a specific day in mind, but now they're on the run we may have inadvertently rushed them along. But that's good because it means they will make mistakes, which gives us the edge in trying to catch the bastards!" Continuing, he added, "Susan and I will take a drive out there tonight and stake the place out."

***

On the drive to the oil pipeline terminal, Harry

and Susan discussed what they knew about the bomber and reasoned that the bomber probably had someone manipulating him and that he was just a pawn in someone else's game.

"The local police are already going house to house in the local town and nearby ranches and farms to ask for help in finding the suspects. They're asking the public to report anything suspicious or anything new they may have seen in the last couple of days. Hopefully, this will stir a few hornets out of their nest and we can find our prey before it stings us!" Harry said.

"Hopefully, the extra police positioned around the terminal will scare off the bombers and we can apprehend them before they get a chance to set off another bomb," Susan said as she took a gulp of lukewarm coffee hoping it would help to keep her awake during their stakeout of the pipeline terminal.

"I was hoping to have an early night tonight," Harry said. Continuing, he added, "I was meant to give my sister a ring tonight, but its way past her bedtime now."

"You're close to your sister then?"

"Yes, but she knows not to ring me, just text me. But she sometimes forgets."

"I don't think we'll see the bomber tonight," Susan said.

"You could be right; it's hard to predict what a criminal will do. They have a different kind of mindset from a normal person. Later tonight, I'll have to have some sleep, otherwise, I can't function," Harry said.

"Me too!"

"We'll give it another hour before we head back to the hotel," Harry said.

"I don't think they'll turn up...not if they have any sense," Susan said.

"Are you fit to drive back tonight?" Harry asked.

"Why?"

"It's a long drive and it's late. We could get a room at a motel," Harry said, smiling.

"Is that your normal chat up line?" Susan asked, laughing.

"No, of course not, I'm so tired you may have to lift into bed…only joking. But seriously, I need a good night's sleep. Do you snore?" Harry said, laughing. A friendship and a possible romance had been developing between Harry and Susan, which was unexpected.

***

Later that night, Singh Ibrahim and Sonia Hermes drove out to the Aurora terminal location and parked several blocks from their target. As they approached their target, Singh suddenly stopped and looked around, it was too quiet, he said to himself. Only the sound of a bird could be heard squawking off in the remote distance.

"Wait! Don't move I don't like the look of this place. Get behind me," Singh said quietly to Sonia. Singh could see in the distance the dark shadow of a person standing by a building. The place had extra security deployed since the bombings, he mused.

Singh then saw a car in the distance drive away with two people inside. He then made his move and planted the bomb where it would do the most damage, he thought. The timer was already set. Then they continued on their journey to their next target.

***

The following morning, Harry and Susan were at the local mobile police headquarters, which was a converted caravan at the terminal when Harry received more information about their suspects from Jamie at the CIA headquarters in Langley, Virginia. Harry was intrigued to learn about the state of mind of his suspects, particularly Mr. Singh Ibrahim.

"Hi, Jamie, what have you got for me?" Harry asked on the phone.

"You'll see on the printout…it covers his early years from a child up to him joining the Marines and to the present day. And the other printout is the background on his girlfriend Miss Sonia Hermes, again from childhood up to the present day."

"Good, speak later," Harry hung up the call.

"He thought, he could take a shortcut…and it didn't work out," Harry remarked.

"What's that?"

"Hmm, yeah…"

"What's that…"

"Oh, it's the background on our Mr Singh Ibrahim. He tried a shortcut and it didn't work out for him. He thought, he could steal and get away with it," Harry said.

"Didn't he know crime doesn't pay?" Susan remarked, smiling.

"Why do people do it, they take the wrong decision and make their lives harder than it already is? What propels people to do it?" Harry asked.

"I don't know."

"My grandfather would always say; always do the right thing because it takes less energy and you don't have to be constantly looking over your shoulder."

"Have you posted more officers around the oil pipeline terminal and had it thoroughly checked over for bombs?" Susan asked the police captain.

"Yes, we've doubled checked the terminal," the police captain replied.

Suddenly, a loud explosion erupted on a freight train as it passed the oil pipeline terminal sending hot shrapnel in all directions and into the large oil storage tanks, which ignited the gas fumes in the storage tanks into a blazing inferno. The mobile police caravan was rocked from side to side like a rocky chair. People ran in all directions not knowing which way to run as panic ensued amongst the crowd, which had gathered that day to see the grand opening of that section of the oil pipeline opened.

Harry lifted himself up and looked out the window of the mobile police headquarters, and was shocked at what he could see. "Shit! I should've prevented this. Are you alright?"

"Yeah, it's not your fault, Harry," Susan muttered as she picked herself up off the floor.

"That bomber is a sly customer, for sure," the police captain said as he picked himself off the floor of the caravan. Continuing, he added, "Fuck! We had electronic phone jamming in operation for this event!"

"Yeah, but it didn't stop the bomber. He took that out of the equation, he used the train as the fuse, and he didn't need to remotely detonate the bomb it was already primed to explode," Harry said authoritatively.

"I'll have every vehicle checked in a ten-mile radius within the next ten minutes and..." the police captain muttered before he was interrupted by Harry.

"It's a waste of time...he's probably well on his way to his next location, I have him leaving the scene of the crime shortly after he planted the bomb on the stationary train late last night. Where he's going...only God knows," Harry said.

"It's like...he's moving up in the world and his actions are getting more sensational," Susan said.

"Yes, and we have to find the bastard before he strikes again," Harry said with a worried tone of voice.

***

"Hi Jamie, run Mr Singh Ibrahim's name with any links to Keystone Oil Pipeline Company or any other links that you think may be useful," Harry said to Jamie at the CIA headquarters.

Susan instantly noticed Harry had directly asked Jamie for his input, usually, it was directed from Harry. Was Harry losing his way in the investigation, she wondered?

"Susan, have you any ideas?" Harry asked intently.

Shaking her head, Susan replied, smiling, "No, I've hit a brick wall, the same as you."

"Well, it's time we sat back and regrouped," Harry said.

"Let's head back to our hotel...our suspects could be anywhere," Harry suggested. On the drive back to their hotel they discussed the case. Harry told Susan that he thought the bomber was being directed by someone else. He felt the bomber had help right from the beginning.

***

The following morning, Harry and Susan discussed their plans for the day over breakfast in the hotel's restaurant. Singh Ibrahim had fooled Harry and Susan into thinking how he would react and Harry had guessed it may be the oil pipeline terminal, which it turned out to be, but by using a passing train as the fuse. Much of the police's efforts to thwart the bomber had gone into watching the oil terminal and not the passing train, which the hot shrapnel from the bomb ignited the terminal gases in the terminal oil storage tanks.

"The bomber wanted us to second guess him, namely me. I made a mistake," Harry said dejectedly.

"My mistake as well, Harry. But, we were both tired by that time in the night," Susan said gleefully.

"Yes, you could be right. These days, I need my beauty sleep!" Harry said, laughing.

"We haven't seen their vehicle since the bombing. We have had no police reports."

"They've no doubt changed vehicles."

"Just come in, Harry. Their vehicle has been located and abandoned sixty miles west of the train bombing," Susan said.

"Hello, chief it's Harry Steel, can you have your boys check out any CCTV footage in a five-minute radius of where our suspects" car was found.

"That's going to take some time!" the police captain replied.

"Yes, I know, but it needs to be done ASAP!" Harry howled down the phone in anger and hung up.

"We'll have to wait until the local police come up with a lead. In the meantime, I'll finish my report to my boss at the CIA," Harry said to Susan.

***

"Hello, Michael it's me Harry Steel, would you like a brief summary of my report?" Harry asked.

"Yes, go ahead." Michael Kurios Director of Counter Intelligence replied.

"I failed. Last night we staked out the oil pipeline terminal, thinking it would be the bomber's target and it was. But, the bomber chose to use a passing train as the fuse as the hot shrapnel from the explosion ignited gases in the oil storage tanks in the terminal. Luckily, no one was killed but there were over a hundred people with serious injuries. We're currently looking for three suspects a Mr Singh Ibrahim, Miss Sonia Hermes and Miss Gina Spinlotti."

Have you used our resources?" Michael asked.

"Yes, Jamie in the basement is currently digging out some information for me," Harry replied.

"What about the cattle mutilations?" Michael asked.

"It's in my report. There's not much to say. I've seen what evidence exists and spoken to the ranchers and farmers. At the moment, I don't have any ideas. It could be a mystery that goes unsolved," Harry remarked.

"What about UFOs and aliens?" Michael asked.

"Not you as well, I was wondering when you would mention the subject," Harry replied.

"What do you mean?"

"It doesn't matter, but tell me why you think its UFOs and aliens that are responsible for the cattle mutilations?" Harry asked.

"I've read the reports from Dr Susan Ginsberg and others who mention the possibility of UFOs and aliens," Michael replied.

Harry could not press his boss for the truth but felt he was holding back the truth. The original file on the case of the cattle mutilations failed to mention anything about UFOs and aliens, he remembered. Harry was now intrigued to know why his boss failed to mention anything about the possibility of UFOs and aliens having a bearing on the case of cattle mutilations, even though, it sounded ridiculous to him.

"Well, until I see evidence to the contrary UFOs and aliens are last in the line of suspects," Harry said.

"Harry, I want you and Dr Ginsberg on a flight to Boston, Massachusetts. The corporate jet will take you there. The file on the case is in your email," Michael said.

"Oh, what about the Nebraska bomber, we're not finished?"

"I understand you're waiting for a lead. Until, then, I need you and Dr Ginsberg on this case. Is that understood?" Michael asked.

"What's the case about?"

"Last night there was a blackout across the whole east coast of America. Find who was responsible," Michael said before hanging up the call.

"What's up?" Susan asked.

"Change of plans, we've got a new mission in Boston, Massachusetts. There was a blackout on the east coast of American last night and we've been reassigned to find out who is responsible," Harry replied. Continuing, he added, "We're to fly out on the corporate jet as soon as possible, like yesterday!"

"What about the Nebraska bomber?"

Harry shrugged his shoulders and said, "I said the same, but they deem this new case important enough to send the corporate jet for us."

Chapter 12

On the flight to Boston, Harry and Susan discussed the facts of the case and both wondered why they had been assigned to the case when the FBI and Homeland Security were already investigating the blackout.

"We're to liaise with local FBI and Homeland Security resources," Harry said.

"What's the reasoning behind that?" Susan asked.

"I'm not sure, but it could be because our boss thinks or knows who's responsible, but needs us to confirm it," Harry said nonchalantly.

***

It was raining and windy when the Learjet landed at Boston airport. Harry and Susan were met by local FBI agents and driven to their hotel and then on to FBI headquarters for a briefing with special agent Delaquez.

"Hi, my name is Harry Steel and this is Dr. Susan Ginsberg."

"Hi, I'm special agent Delaquez. I understand that the CIA is to liaise with us and Homeland Security on this case?" Delaquez asked inquisitively.

"Yes, you can have all the glory…and the paperwork," Harry replied, smiling.

Delaquez nodded his head and said, "Good, we know where we stand." Continuing, he added, "Last night the entire east coast suffered a power outage and the blackout lasted all night. According to the Boston Energy Company, they said it was down to a rogue software glitch, which is yet to be verified. This caused a substation to fail, which then had a domino effect down the line resulting in the blackout. Currently, large sections along the east coast are still without power.

Luckily, for us, we are served by another power station when the other is offline, so we were only without power for a few hours, while they fixed the substation."

"What is the name of the power station?" Harry asked intently.

"The NextEra Energy Seabrook nuclear power station, which is located near the town of Seabrook, New Hampshire. It's about forty miles north from Boston." Delaquez replied.

"Could this blackout be the actions of a computer hacker?" Susan asked intently.

"Not according to the power company."

"Okay, thanks for your help; we'll be on our way."

"There's a CIA vehicle in the car park waiting for you," Delaquez said.

***

"Let's take a drive to the power station and see what they have to say," Harry said to Susan.

"Yes, please!" Susan said rhetorically. She felt the same as Harry and was not pleased to be plucked from the pinnacle of a case when it seemed they were close to catching the bombers. To her it was madness and to Harry, it was insane, especially when the net was closing in on the bombers. It would only be a matter of time before the bombers made a mistake and revealed their location, Susan and Harry thought.

In the meantime, what did you think of Delaquez?" Harry asked.

"Someone who thinks he's the boss," Susan said. She knew the rivalry between the CIA and the FBI was legendary and sometimes egos got in the way.

"Exactly, what I thought," Harry said.

"Do you plan to share what we find out?"

"Not until I have to," Harry replied nonchalantly.

***

Later that afternoon, Harry and Susan's vehicle approached the entrance to the Seabrook nuclear power station and stopped at the security gate. Harry and Susan flashed their CIA credentials at the security guard, and then the guard checked for authorisation to let them in. They had an appointment to see the head of operations that afternoon.

"Hello, my name is Phillip Mowbray head of day to day operations."

"My name is Harry Steel and this Dr. Susan Ginsberg. Can you tell us what caused the blackout last night?" Harry asked.

"Our technicians are working on that at the moment and they believe it was a software error that runs part of the electricity grid. This caused part of the electricity grid to fail all along the east coast," Mowbray replied.

"When will you know for sure whether it was a software error or something else?" Harry asked.

"By the end of the week, we should have a better idea," Mowbray replied.

"At the time of the blackout, were you generating electricity?" Susan asked.

"Yes, all our nuclear reactors were online. We didn't shut down anything. You just can't switch a nuclear reactor off by a flick of a switch, it takes time. We continued to produce electricity, while the blackout lasted," Mowbray replied sharply.

"What happens to the electricity you produced in the blackout?" Harry asked.

"It goes to its link in the grid and dissipates if the link is broken. It's not like you can switch the electricity to another part of the grid because of the way the grid is designed to be a fixed structure. That's why you see whole areas lose their power until that part of the grid is repaired. It's not like the structure of the Internet infrastructure where you can route Internet traffic to different routers and avoid a blockage," Mowbray replied. Continuing, he added, "Let me show you the nuclear reactors."

Harry and Susan followed the operations director to the nuclear reactor hub. In the nuclear reactor hub, they saw how the uranium rods were cooled by giant intakes of seawater that kept the reactors working normally. He explained that some of that water is super-heated by the uranium rods into steam that is then used to turn the turbine blades of the turbines, which then creates electricity.

Then the operations director showed Harry and Susan the turbine hall where they saw six massive turbines and heard the humming sound of their blades turning to create the electricity generated by the power station.

"What happens if you lose power in a power outage?" Susan asked.

"We have backup diesel engines to generate electricity to work our pumps and other key devices, which keep the nuclear reactors in a good state, should that occur," Mowbray replied matter-of-factly.

"Oh, I see…"

"Did that happen last night?" Harry asked intently.

"No, we had no power outage here…it was a nearby substation we believe caused the blackout. We had our own electricity to manage our water pumps and other key equipment," Mowbray replied.

"Did you have any other unusual activity last night?" Harry asked intently.

"Yes, we had reports of strange lights seen in the

sky," Mowbray replied.

"Argh!" Harry muttered as he looked on in disbelief at Susan who just shrugged her shoulders and sighed.

"Some of our staff witnessed a strange light hovering over one of the nuclear reactors just before the blackout occurred," Mowbray replied.

"And what time was that?"

"Around eight just before the blackout, which started about fifteen minutes later," Mowbray replied matter-of-factly.

"Can I speak to those witnesses?" Harry asked intently.

"Yes. There's Bob and Bill down in maintenance and the security guard at the front gate." Mowbray replied. Continuing, he added, "I believe some more staff saw the light...I'll have to check."

***

"You saw a strange light hovering over the nuclear reactors last night, is that correct?" Harry asked intently.

"Yes, Bob and I both saw the light at the same time," Bill said.

"What shape was it?"

"The shape was like a UFO...saucer shape and it just hovered for about twenty minutes over the reactors. And then just disappeared into thin air, it just vanished. One minute it was there and the next it was gone," Bill replied.

"The security guard saw the same," Bob muttered.

"Is there anything else to add?" Harry asked.

"No, that's it."

"And you Bob?"

"No, that's it."

"Have either one of you seen strange lights over the power station before this occasion?" Harry asked intently.

"Yes, we have…"

"When was that and did it result in a blackout?" Harry asked sharply.

"Yes it did, but it was a while ago now…say about three years ago now. I remember because both Bob and I witnessed the event, but we didn't relate the two events together. So we paid no attention to the lights and never reported the lights because they were not directly over the power station at the time. Besides, it would not be a good move to report seeing a UFO because there's still is a stigma associated with reporting UFOs," Bill said and Bob nodded in agreement.

"So it was a UFO what you saw?" Harry asked intently.

"Yes, how else would you describe what we saw?"

Harry shrugged his shoulders and asked, "What sort of shape were the lights?"

"From our position, it looked cigar-shaped at first, but the lights moved slightly and we could see it was saucer-shaped. The classic flying saucer shape is how I would describe it. It was similar to what we saw the other night over the nuclear reactor. That night we were closer to the UFO and could see clearly its shape and size," Bob said and Bill nodded in agreement.

"What size do you think it was?"

"I was trying to work that out by comparing it to the length of the reactor hub, which I believe is around a hundred feet long. It looked as though it was easily the same sort of size. Yes, I would say around one hundred feet in diameter would be my estimate," Bill said.

"Would you agree Bob?"

"Yes, that sounds about right."

"Did you notice any markings on the UFO or anything else?" Harry asked intently.

"No, didn't see any. Did you see any Bill?"

"No."

"Well, thanks for your help lads."

"Oh, by the way, do you think the UFO had anything to do with the blackout? Bill asked.

"I haven't seen any evidence to prove they did," Harry replied sharply.

"Thanks for your help," Susan said.

"Okay, Mr Mowbray we'll speak to the security guard on the way out. Thanks for your help," Harry said.

On the way out, Harry and Susan stopped at the security gate to speak to the security guard.

"You saw some strange lights last night, is that correct?" Harry asked.

"Yes, it was shaped like the saucer shape UFO and lasted for about twenty minutes. It then just vanished before the blackout began minutes later," the security guard replied.

"Did you see any markings on the UFO last night?" Harry asked intently.

"No, can't say I did it was too far away to see anything like that from where I was stationed here at the security gate," the security guard replied.

"Have you seen other lights before?" Susan asked.

"Or have you seen any other strange occurrences?" Harry asked interrupting.

"Hmm, yes, but I never reported it because they were not over the power station. A similar type of lights in the past, but never hovering over the nuclear reactors like last night," the security guard replied.

"Did those lights you saw ever coincide with

blackouts?"

"No, never...as far as I can remember," the security guard replied.

"Is there anything else you wish to say on the matter?" Susan asked.

"No, I think I've told you everything," the security guard replied.

Chapter 13

At the CIA headquarters in Langley, Virginia a top-level meeting was about to take place in a secure room on the third floor of the building. Paul Henderson Director of the CIA had gathered the six department chiefs to discuss the latest developments.

"Good evening ladies and gentlemen we are here to discuss the recent blackout that occurred last night all along the east coast of America. Normally, the blackout would be an issue for Homeland Security or the FBI, but as you know we're involved because it may have been caused by our enemies. This is currently being investigated by agents of the CIA to establish the facts. Michael's department is currently leading this investigation and will now give us an update on progress," Paul Henderson Director of the CIA said.

"Currently I have two agents in the field assessing the facts about the blackout. It's too soon to give an explicit answer, but I have to inform you that a UFO saucer shape light was seen hovering over the nuclear reactors at the Seabrook power station, which is situated around forty miles north of Boston, Massachusetts, on the east coast. My leading agent says the UFO light appeared for twenty minutes around fifteen minutes before the blackout occurred." Michael Kurios Director of Counter Intelligence said.

"What is your agent's conclusion?" Paul Henderson Director of the CIA asked.

"It's too early to call. But it looks like our enemies are up to their usual antics. I'm having a task to conceal the truth from my agents Harry Steel and Dr. Susan Ginsberg. They're starting to doubt my actions, even though they've followed every order," Michael Kurios replied.

"Do you believe you can keep the truth from them?" Paul Henderson Director of the CIA asked.

"Yes, at the moment, but holding the lid on the pot is one thing but stopping it from boiling over is another. The more cases that my agents experience with the talk of UFOs, in the mixing pot, then the more it will become increasingly difficult to hide the truth from them. These agents are not stupid they are highly trained, intelligent and they can spot a rat without trying. I also hate lying because it puts my agents' lives at risk," Michael Kurios replied.

"None of us here like lying, but it's a necessary evil until we're ready to reveal to the world where we stand on the issue. Until that time, we all have to maintain the status quo," Paul Henderson Director of the CIA said.

"Well, it's best if you keep it that way. The fewer people, who know the truth the better, we can't afford the secret to spill out of control, at least, until we're ready," General John Schneider Director of Operations said sternly.

"When do you think we will be ready to match our foe?" Michael Kurios asked intently.

Shrugging his shoulders and leaning forward on the table, General Schneider said, "At the moment, we're going as fast as we can safely go."

"What do we do if it turns out our suspicions are correct?" Ruth Gillingham Director of Internal Affairs asked.

"There's not a lot we can do until we're ready to react," General John Schneider said forcibly.

"That's right, we can't afford to provoke our enemies until we're ready," Paul Henderson said.

"Will you be able to keep Harry Steel inline, without revealing the truth? Ruth Gillingham Director of

Internal Affairs asked.

"Yes, he will be fine," Michael Kurios replied succinctly.

"How long do we have to continue with this charade…when will we be ready to act against our enemies?" Anthony Pagilia Director of Espionage asked incredulously.

"Within the next eighteen months…maybe sooner if all goes to plan," General John Schneider replied optimistically.

"When will it be safe to inform the public?" George Hammond Director of Communications asked intently. He wanted to inform the public before the story broke piecemeal and they were flat-footed into providing answers. He knew it would be a risk to inform the public, but thought the risk not to inform the public was greater.

"At the last possible moment…is probably the short answer. It's anyone's guess when it's the best time to inform the public," Paul Henderson replied. He knew from studies carried out secretly on public reaction to that kind of news that it would most likely provoke all-out anarchy across the country if not the world.

"Would it be best if we informed the public now, when we may have time to get stronger, while we deal with some public anarchy?" Julia Hayward Director of Special Operations asked.

"You're right, but I don't know how the government will see it? No one likes to think their actions could cause a total collapse of the government," Paul Henderson replied. Continuing, he added, "Let's have a show of hands."

Paul looked around the table and it was fifty, fifty, and his casting vote would seal the action. "It's evenly divided between you, but I sigh with no for now. The reason is now doesn't feel right…right now. For many reasons such as our readiness to react to our enemies, our best guess could be up to eighteen months' time before we're ready. So for now, we keep the public in the dark." Paul was not about to rock the status quo even if there was a consensus amongst his directors for full disclosure. He was glad that for now the secrecy would be maintained until the time was right for the public to know the truth. He was not even sure the vast majority of the public could handle the truth because it went against everything the public had been told about the enemy. For now, the CIA would keep the truth well and truly hidden until it was ready to reveal all to the believers and the non-believers. Society did not need another thing to upset its delicate balance between peace and anarchy.

Chapter 14

Meanwhile, the following morning, Ibrahim had just stolen a white transit van for his next terrorist act. He had read and seen the news about the blackout and the appearance of strange lights over the nuclear reactors at the Seabrook power station. He had decided to make the journey from Nebraska to the East Coast. He had a plan and the means to carry it out.

"How do we get into the power station…there sure to have security on the gate?" Sonia Hermes asked. Mrs Gina Spinlotti looked on in amazement.

"Simple, we overpower the security guard," Ibrahim replied.

The two women winced, but looked on in amazement, at the thought of physical contact with the security guard at the power station.

"How do we do that?" Sonia asked in disbelief.

"Don't worry, I'll figure it out before we get there," Ibrahim replied.

"You don't expect us to overpower the security guard?" Miss Gina Spinlotti asked incredulously.

"Yes, doesn't the sparrow entice the worm with its song? Don't worry; before we arrive, I'll have worked out a plan. In the meantime, keep your mind on the traffic and avoid arousing any suspicions from the police. We don't want to announce our arrival, now do we?" Ibrahim replied.

"I'll turn into the next motel I see along the highway," Gina said nonchalantly.

"Yes, do," Ibrahim said, smiling. Continuing, he added, "What about you, Sonia? Do you feel like a rest stop?"

"Yeah, need a rest stop like…I'm dying of thirst," Sonia replied.

"There's one just up ahead…looks okay."

"Good, I'll take care of business, while you wait," Ibrahim said.

***

Later that night, they sat in their motel room discussing the events surrounding the blackout of the East Coast.

"What do you think about the strange lights that are seen at the nuclear power station moments before the blackout started?" Gina asked.

"I haven't thought about it until now. Not much to say, but ask the aliens or some secret government black op programme you should contact," Ibrahim said, smiling.

"Why do you ask?" Sonia asked patiently.

"Just talking…that's all. I never expected to be on the run from the police."

"You're not getting cold feet are you?"

"No, just worried about getting caught before we get a chance to strike. What about you?" Gina asked.

"Shit! I hope we have a good escape worked into our plan," Sonia replied.

***

The following day, it was raining heavily as Singh Ibrahim and the women continued their journey towards Boston in their stolen transit van.

"What are you planning for the power station?" Gina asked sheepishly.

"Yes, what are your plans?" Sonia asked eagerly

"Don't worry girls… I've got a plan of action. In the meantime, keep your mind on the road. We've still got a lot of hours driving before we hit Boston," Singh said matter-of-factly.

Chapter 15

Meanwhile, Harry Steel was on the phone with his boss Michael Kurios briefing him on the latest progress.

"We have no idea what caused the power outage other than plausible ideas. The technicians considered it to be a software problem and have replaced or rebooted devices in the electricity grid. The idea of aliens and flying saucers having any involvement in the blackout is possible, but I saw no evidence to suggest so. But, I don't think you've been honest with me from the start. I've noticed it around three months ago. So, what's going on?" Harry asked intently.

Michael sighed and winced at the thought of telling the truth, but they were friends not just work colleagues.

"Yes, there's more, but not over the phone," Michael replied.

"Well, that just about wraps it up for now and I'll make my way back to the office," Harry said.

"Yes, of course," Michael said before ending the call.

***

"Shut the door!"

"Take a seat, Harry. Over the past three months or more we are confident our enemy has been orchestrating events to weaken our defences," Michael Kurios said.

"Who are the enemy?" Harry asked eagerly.

"Only a few people know this but the force responsible for the flying saucers! I know you don't believe it, nor did I, until I saw the evidence. It could be the Chinese, North Koreans or the Russians or another country twenty-five years ahead of our technology. It's happened before when the Nazis had technology far ahead of us during the Second World War," Michael replied.

"So, it's not an alien force?" Harry asked incredulously.

"We're not sure, it's possible, but whoever they are we believe their technology is at least twenty-five years ahead of us," Michael said.

"No shit!"

Harry was stunned at the news. But, he knew he had been right about not being told the truth about his recent missions. And now he knew the truth, he wondered what nation could be behind the flying saucer mysteries, he said to himself.

"In the meantime, keep it under wraps," Michael said quietly.

"Okay boss," Harry said as he stood up and walked out of the office and made his way back down to his office on the first floor, which had a panoramic view of the river. He needed to assess the new information to his current missions.

Looking out at the meandering river as it passed the nearby farming complex, Harry considered the new information. An unknown enemy was at work in many of his current missions. The enemy's agenda was unknown at present. Michael had been scant on detail or knew more but was unwilling to tell the complete truth, he said to himself.

The recent blackout, the radar detections, the Ebola outbreaks and the cattle mutilations all have links to the enemy, whoever they are? But, it all started to make sense to Harry as he mulled over the evidence in his mind. He grimaced at the thought of being another entity's slave. Whatever the enemy's agenda was and their reasons were it now seemed almost academic because none of it looked good for mankind. It felt like we were the pawns in a game of chess. It felt like they were probing and testing our resources for an ultimate battle, he said to himself.

***

The following morning, Harry Steel had breakfast with Dr. Susan Ginsberg at the hotel in Boston, close to the old port complex and briefed Susan that the CIA believed the Russians, North Koreans or the Chinese were behind the flying saucer phenomena.

"I believe many of the top echelons of power believe it's the Chinese who are our enemy and not some aliens from another planet," Harry said nonchalantly.

"You believe it's the Chinese and not the North Koreans or the Russians?" Susan asked incredulously.

"Yes, why not…we don't understand them just like the Russians," Harry replied. Continuing, he added, "Whoever the enemy are we'll have to deal with it one way or the other."

"How does this news affect our investigation?" Susan asked intently.

Harry shrugged his shoulders and said, "Well, at least, we know who'll be the likely culprits either the Russians, North Koreans or the Chinese? If I was a betting man and I'm not, then my money is on the Chinese."

"Why the Chinese and not another country are the culprits?" Susan asked intently.

"I don't understand them and I think they have a complicated written language. And they have shown with their 5G mobile phone network how far advanced they are against our current technology. So, yeah, the Chinese would seem the culprit and not the Russians or the North Koreans because we would've heard about it long ago," Harry replied.

"What about the blackout?" Susan asked.

"Well, if the energy company technicians can't find the glitch in the grid then perhaps we can lay the blame on our enemy. We need to make another visit and see the operations manager again," Harry said, smiling. Continuing, he added, "Let's take a drive out there."

***

"Hi there, we need to ask you some more questions."

"Yes, go ahead," the operations manager replied.

"Did your technicians find the problem with the blackout?" Harry asked intently.

"Yes and no. Yes, we found the broken link in the electricity grid but found no error in the device. But, we replaced it just the same and rebooted the software. Everything is working as it should be. You should remember the state of Massachusetts uses twice as much electricity as the state currently produces. So, it's easy for a power outage to occur in a fragmented grid that needs to be updated for the needs of the people along the east coast," the operations manager replied.

"Do you think those strange UFO lights seen hovering over the nuclear reactors had anything to do with the power outage and the blackout along the east coast the other night?" Harry asked.

Shrugging his shoulders, the operations manager replied, "It's possible, but I don't know how…it's beyond me."

Harry and Susan just looked at each other for a reaction. Both felt it could be a possibility, but neither was willing to commit to the idea.

"Didn't we cover these questions before?" the operations manager asked curiously.

"Why didn't you make a report of the incident?" Susan asked intently ignoring the previous reply.

The operations manager grimaced at the thought of being extensively interrogated as he tried to find the answers to Harry's and Susan's questions.

"It didn't make sense to report UFO sightings…it would've been seen as a bad career move, so I didn't bother," the operations manager said.

"Can I speak to the technicians that repaired the substation?" Harry asked.

"Yes, of course, I'll phone ahead and get them here," the operations manager replied.

***

Later that morning, Harry and Susan sat down in the canteen of the power station to interview the two technicians that repaired the faulty substation.

"We found the broken link in the grid, but we found no faulty device or software, but we replaced the device and rebooted the software at that substation, just the same," the technician said.

"Why the substation failed is a mystery?" the second technician asked.

"Did you see any strange lights or any other strange phenomena that night?" Harry asked intently.

"No, we were both indoors working at the time…lights were seen hovering over the nuclear reactors that night. But, I've seen or we both have over the years seen strange lights around the power station," the technician replied.

"Many times, over the years, but we didn't make a report because we don't want the ridicule. So, we avoid it like the plague," the other technician said.

"Have these strange lights coincided with power outages and blackouts before?

"Yes, sometimes they have, but not exactly at the same time."

"Which is it?"

"We've both seen strange lights sometimes near the time of a blackout. But, you have to remember blackouts don't happen every week or month. They occasionally happen from a power outage or a storm that has knocked out part of the grid infrastructure. We spend most of our time out and about repairing the grid infrastructure. Usually, it's the switchgear in a substation that gets shorted," the technician replied.

"How does a power outage occur?" Susan asked intently.

"There're many ways, but usually from a sudden increase or decrease in the load on the power line. Think of it like a river that sometimes floods," the technician replied.

"Okay, thanks for your help," Harry and Susan said as they watched the men get back to their work in the maintenance hall, which was situated at the back of the turbine room at right angles to the canteen room they were situated in.

"The last part of the tour is the pumping station, which keeps the uranium rods from overheating and is critical to the safe production of electricity from nuclear power," the operations manager said.

"How much water does it need to operate?" Harry asked curiously.

"A lot...that's why we're situated right next to the sea, without the water to cool the rods and the reactor...the reactor would explode and cause an environmental disaster. Similar to what happened at Fukushima Daiichi Nuclear Power Plant in Japan just recently," the operations manager replied.

"Do you have backup plans?" Susan asked.

"Yes, there are plans in place should the pumping station fail," the operations manager replied matter-of-factly.

"Such as…?"

Shrugging his shoulders, the operations manager said, "We can manually divert water straight to the reactor should both pumps fail, but this would take time to set up. It's been assessed in the recent risk assessment. Everything was reassessed after 'nine eleven' when we got attacked without warning."

"Yes, you're right."

"We got caught napping on 'nine eleven' and ever since then there's heightened security on everything like we're taking no chances," the operations manager said gleefully.

"Where is the pumping station?" Susan asked as she turned around from the table to look out the window of the canteen.

"It's on the left-hand side of the reactor looking out to the sea. From here it's straight through that wall and about fifteen feet to the left attached to the back of the reactor room and about twenty feet lower than where we're standing now," the operations manager said.

Suddenly, the canteen windows blew apart and everyone inside was shaken by the nearby explosion.

"Look!"

"It's the pumping station!" the operations manager shouted out.

Harry and Susan could see the damage to the pumping station building, which had been torn apart by the explosion. To Harry, it had all the hallmarks of a high explosives discharge.

"That was no accident!" the operations manager said.

"Yeah, no shit," someone in the canteen muttered.

Everyone could see the twisted metal and the destruction of the pumping station, which was now not providing the cooling water needed to keep the reactors from overheating and it exploding.

While the operations manager was busy organising the backup water supply to the reactor another explosion blew apart the remote backup water supply junction. It was now a race against time as the nuclear reactor would continue to rise in temperature close to another Fukushima Daiichi Nuclear Disaster event within hours.

Harry and Susan found the security guard tied up and willing and able to describe the bombers as two women and a man. After several more questions, Harry and Susan were sure they were the same culprits they had failed to catch the week before.

"The bomber has raised the stakes!"

"Yes, without doubt," Susan agreed.

"The Homeland Security and the FBI are already processing the scene. The bomb squad are sweeping the area for any other devices," Harry said.

"We have to catch these terrorists before they strike again," Susan said intently.

"I have the local police checking CCTV cameras trying to locate the vehicle they used to get here and out, and so far, they lose track of their vehicle five miles from here," Harry said. Continuing, he added, "It looks like they've switched vehicles in an area where they were no cameras about."

"Clever bastards," Susan muttered.

"Yeah, I was just thinking that. And now we must think of another way we can catch these culprits," Harry suggested.

"What ideas do you have?"

"None, until I speak to our boss," Harry remarked.

***

"Hello, Harry what's happening!" Michael Kurios asked. Continuing, he added, "I heard on the news about the explosion and what's the situation there?"

"Susan and I are just about finished here, we were about to get started looking for the terrorists when you sent me the text message to get in touch," Harry said.

"Is it under control there?" Michael asked intently.

"The operations manager said they have a few hours before the reactor blows, so there busy trying to rig up some temporary water pipelines to the reactor. And I believe it's the same bombers from Nebraska," Harry replied.

Michael winced at the news from Harry about how serious the potential for a nuclear disaster was. "Let me have a report as soon as possible," Michael said before hanging up the call.

***

Within a few minutes, Harry was on his mobile replying to an urgent text message from his sister.

"Hello, it's me, what's the news?" Harry asked intently.

"Harry, the results from the laboratory are here," Rebecca replied.

"What are the results?"

"The same as the other two tests…none human!" Rebecca replied.

Harry winced at the news; he just didn't believe what his sister was telling him, even though he did not doubt her words.

***

Later that day, at the hotel bar in Boston, Harry and Susan discussed the case. It was now urgent to find the bombers before they could strike again.

"What's on your mind, Harry?" Susan asked.

Shrugging his shoulders, Harry said, "I've calculated that the bombers would've used up the C4 explosives they originally had. So, unless they have another source of explosives at hand, we can be sure they're holding up somewhere waiting to disappear into the mist."

"We know they changed vehicles shortly after leaving the power station, but where they're going is a mystery," Susan said.

Grimacing at the thought, Harry said, "Yeah, which had been pre-planned in my view."

"Can we be sure of your calculations? Susan asked in disbelief.

"Right now, I'm not sure of anything except for death and taxes," Harry replied nonchalantly.

"What do you mean by that," Susan asked incredulously.

"Listen! To what I've to say, all my recent missions have involved the mention of flying saucers and aliens in some form. Now, our boss hasn't been telling me the truth. So, I expect there's more to the story than he has been willing to tell me. Do I believe in flying saucers and aliens...not until I see evidence will I believe that's the case," Harry replied.

"Didn't you say it was the Chinese or another country twenty-five years ahead of ours?" Susan asked.

"Yes, that's right. I need another JD and coke." Harry muttered calmly.

"If it helps I'll have another drink," Susan sighed with a soft tone of voice.

"It sometimes pays to sit back and relax and think about the mission without going full throttle into a disaster," Harry said philosophically with a wry smile across his face. His experience had taught him not to panic.

"Yeah, I agree, but how do we find the bombers?" Susan asked tentatively.

"I thought, you'd never ask," Harry replied, smiling. Continuing, he added, "Someone will make a mistake, it's only a matter of time. I've Langley analysing the local CCTV footage against their profiles. A camera in a gas station or a food shop is my guess where we'll get a break in the case."

"Yeah, everyone has to eat."

"Sooner or later, someone will make a mistake. Remember, it takes time to crunch all that data and then to make a match in a database."

"Would you like another drink," the hotel bar waitress asked.

"Would you like another drink, Susan?"

"Yes, a Long Island Ice Tea for me."

"And for me a JD and coke…thanks."

"What are our plans for tomorrow?" Susan asked.

Shrugging his shoulders, Harry replied, "Not a lot we can do until we get a break in the case. But, I feel we will because fate always intervenes."

"What do you mean?"

"Well, it brought us together," Harry replied, smiling.

"Fate had its way before we got started," Susan said, smiling.

***

Meanwhile, Mr Singh Ibrahim and his two female collaborators were searching for a place to hide out when they came across an old abandoned coal mining operation.

"This is ideal, we can hide the van in those outbuildings and find a place to rest up in that building over there," Ibrahim said as he pointed to a building with the least damage to its windows.

"Looks cool to me," Sonia said.

"Tomorrow, we figure out our escape route. Tonight, we rest and take stock of the situation," Ibrahim said.

"I reckon we make a move as soon as possible," Gina Spinlotti said.

"There you go again already starting to panic," Sonia suggested.

"First thing we need...is to find another vehicle...they probably already have our current van in their system," Ibrahim said.

"You didn't have to spend time with that creepy security guard?" Gina muttered.

"What do you suggest?"

"We have to disappear into the ether before we have more heat to handle. Tomorrow, we lose the cops and drive down to South Carolina and from there go our separate ways," Ibrahim said calmly.

"What's in South Carolina?"

"I have a place there where we can hold up for a while before we all go our separate ways," Ibrahim replied.

"How do get there unseen?" Sonia asked with an anxious tone of voice.

"Yes, how do we get there?" Gina also asked.

"Don't worry girls, I've it all figured out," Ibrahim replied forcibly.

"Well, well, good for you, but are you gonna tell us...or you just gonna sit there with a big smile on your face?" Gina asked incredulously.

"I'll tell you in the morning, in the meantime, get some sleep and rest," Ibrahim replied.

***

The following morning, Ibrahim outlined his plan to the girls. He explained that he would call a taxi with a fake reason for the ride. He said that they had broken down after visiting the old coal mine that morning and would require a lift to the nearest garage. He explained they would use the taxi to get to another place where they could switch vehicles without being seen by CCTV cameras. The taxi driver would be tied up until we decided to inform the police; he explained that they would leave false information for the police to follow with the taxi driver. Ibrahim explained that using this ruse they would be able to get to South Carolina before the police found the abandoned taxi vehicle.

"We now need the best place to find another car to switch to without being seen by any CCTV cameras," Ibrahim said. Continuing, he added, "Any ideas?"

"Have you run out of ideas already Singh?" Gina muttered.

"Oh, he's been right so far," Sonia declared.

"What if we use the taxi and clean it up?"

"I just thought you girls would have some ideas. I have an idea which just may work. If we drive into the long-stay carpark at the nearest airport and switch cars there then if we are lucky it would be perhaps several weeks before they find the car. I believe this is the plan," Ibrahim replied.

Suddenly, they could hear the sound of birds squawking as a car approached their building and stopped just outside the front door. They peered outside through the cracked broken windows at the SUV as an old man got out of the car and slowly made his way to the front entrance. The old man was heading their way straight for the front entrance when the old man, suddenly turned and saw their van parked inside the adjacent building.

"Hello, hello…this is private property!" the old man called out.

"Turn around…while we search you," Ibrahim said calmly from behind the front door as the old man began to raise his hands.

The old man was shocked to see Singh and the girls; he was expecting to see teenagers using the place to party. After the girls searched the old man for any firearms they tied him to a chair.

Ibrahim then discussed what to do with the old man. He did not want to change his plans but felt there was no choice, but to change his plans. He felt fate had played its card for him. Singh played his card and let it be known to the captive that they were on their way to Chattanooga, Tennessee. He had previously quietly told Sonia to let the cat out of the bag.

"How long will it take to get to Chattanooga?" Sonia asked.

"Shut the fuck up, I hope he didn't hear that," Ibrahim said. Continuing, he added, "Shut the fucking door!"

"We'll be there and gone before they find this old man," Ibrahim said. Continuing, he added, "Just enough time to pick up the explosives and disappear."

"More explosives…?" Sonia asked.

"Yeah, I haven't finished yet," Ibrahim replied. Continuing, he added, "Make sure this guy is tied up where he can't make a play."

"Let's get going before the cops turn up unexpectedly."

"Yeah, let's get the hell out of here," Sonia said.

"Make sure the van is well undercover and we'll keep to our plan," Ibrahim suggested.

***

On the outskirts of the local airport, they pulled

into a long stay carpark and waited for an unsuspecting victim to park their car before going on holiday.

Now, we have switched cars, we can only hope the owners of this car are going on a lengthy holiday," Sonia said.

"Stop at the nearest gas station, we don't want to run out of gas before we get to Head Island," Ibrahim demanded.

"What about the old man at the coal mine?" Gina asked.

Now, make sure you don't look up to any CCTV cameras while you buy some food and pay for the gas Sonia," Ibrahim said. Continuing, he added, "He'll be alright for a couple of days...we'll ring the cops before the old man dies of thirst."

"We should've just shot him, so he doesn't get a chance to foil our plans," Gina said.

"No need, we need him to give the cops the wrong information...and besides, I don't like to shoot someone in cold blood it goes against the grain," Ibrahim said.

"But, you don't mind blowing people up!"

"Yeah, something like that."

"It's too late in the day to get squeamish," Sonia muttered.

"I'm not, just pointing to the obvious that's all," Gina said.

Chapter 16

Meanwhile, Paul Henderson Director at CIA headquarters, in Langley, Virginia, the USA and was about to convene a meeting with division heads.

"Good morning, ladies and gentlemen. The enemy we believe is testing our defences. The recent power outage along the east coast is a recent example. Our fragmented electricity grid is prone to fail due to the underfunding of key infrastructure upgrades. We also know about the Ebola outbreaks and other attacks in Africa. We're here today, to discuss, our next move," Paul Henderson Director of the CIA said.

"But, this is not news!" Ruth Gillingham Director of Internal Affairs stressed. She had heard it all before and wanted to keep the status quo.

"Yes, but the frequency is!" Paul Henderson replied. Continuing, he added, "Our enemy has upped the stakes and we have to be ready."

"The frequency is our problem because it shows the signs of an imminent attack," General John Schneider Director of Operations said as he leaned forward on the table.

"Are we capable of matching their technology?" Julia Hayward Director of Special Operations asked with scepticism in her tone of voice.

"We have to; otherwise, we become their slaves." General Schneider replied.

"Do we have the technology?" Julia Hayward asked again.

"Yes and no. Most of the new technology is not fully tested," General Schneider replied.

"At some point, they will force our hand, and we will end up in a war," Paul Henderson said.

"Our intelligence suggests our enemy is getting

ready to attack. We may have only months before they launch a full-on attack on us," Michael Kurios Director of Counter Intelligence stressed.

"Should we inform the public?" George Hammond Director of Communications asked.

"Sooner or later, we may have no choice but to inform the public. I think it's time we did inform the public before it's too late. The conspiracy theorists are having a field day with their disinformation and millions of people believe them," Julia Hayward Director of Special Operations replied.

"You're right, Julia. I think it's about time we did inform the public in a limited way," Anthony Pagilia Director of Espionage said.

"How do we inform the public without causing total mayhem?" General Schneider asked.

"That's the million-dollar question, just how do we do it?" Anthony Pagilia Director of Espionage asked.

"Before we can inform the public, we'll need the approval from the president," Paul Henderson Director of the CIA said. Continuing, he added, "This may be harder to achieve than you think and don't forget the president is up for re-election and may have other fish to fry."

"So, what are you suggesting Paul?" Anthony Pagilia Director of Espionage asked.

"I can take the case to the president and see what he says. But, I have my doubts about his ability to see the wider picture because he's up for re-election and this may cloud his judgement. If the president loses the election then we'll have to wait several months before a new president is installed and in control in the White House. But, first, we need to discuss how we propose to inform the public," Paul Henderson Director of the CIA said.

"Perhaps it's best if we get the president to make a public announcement," Michael Kurios Director of Counter Intelligence said.

"That's one possibility," Paul Henderson said.

"Perhaps, we should first inform the public that UFOs do exist and that an alien force is on our planet," General John Schneider Director of Operations said.

"Perhaps it's best if we keep the status quo and wait for our enemy to act before we unleash the devil," Ruth Gillingham Director of Internal Affairs said.

"I understand your view Ruth, but I don't think we have the luxury of just keeping the status quo. Our enemy has upped the stakes in its frequency of attacks and we need to prepare the public for what may come next," Paul Henderson said.

"We run the risk of being outsmarted before we get a chance of responding adequately to the threat if we don't inform the public somehow," General John Schneider Director of Operations stressed.

"Do you have a suggestion on how we do that General?" Ruth Gillingham asked.

"Yes, we create a leak and the information then becomes public," General Schneider replied.

"That's another possibility, which has merit," Paul Henderson said.

"We have to be careful we don't start a riot that we can't stop. Perhaps, we can inform the public through the use of leaks to the press," Anthony Pagilia Director of Espionage said.

"If the president makes an announcement then it's possible that half the population in America will not believe what the president says. The public may see it as fake news. I suggest we orchestrate a series of leaks, which we can confirm," Julia Hayward Director of Special Operations said.

"Julia, it may come to that if the president doesn't see sense," Paul Henderson said.

"I agree, this may be our only option should the president resist our advice," George Hammond Director of Communications said. Continuing, he added, "Whatever we decide then we better get on with it because our enemy could strike at any moment."

"Okay are there any more thoughts on the matter at hand before we take a vote," Paul Henderson said as he looked around the table at the faces of his colleagues.

"Yes, Michael what's on your mind?" Paul Henderson asked.

"Before we inform the public we should inform our staff of our position. In fact, the whole organisation needs to know the truth," Michael Kurios Director of Counter Intelligence said.

"Yes, of course, but the president needs to be informed of our plans before that happens. I know you have had trouble recently convincing your agent Harry Steel of the situation, but the president needs to give his approval first and if that doesn't happen we'll discuss further what we should do," Paul Henderson said. Continuing, he added, "Let's see a show of hands for the action to inform the public."

Paul Henderson looked around the table and only Ruth had her hand down with a visible frown across her face showing her dislike for the proposed action. Everyone else was in favour of informing the public either through an announcement by the president or by a series of leaks to the press.

"I'll convene another meeting after I've briefed the president," Paul Henderson said before ending the meeting.

Chapter 17

Later that day, Paul Henderson Director of the CIA was sat on the back seat of his chauffeur-driven car being driven to the White House. Inside the Oval Office, the president of the USA was sat behind his highly polished oak and mahogany desk, which had been a gift from the British Monarchy. Sat on both sides of the president was his Chief of Staff Felix Gardner and his Secretary of State Jerry Lauder and Paul Henderson was sat opposite the president.

"Good afternoon, Mr President. I'm here today to brief you on issues relating to national security. You are aware of the recent blackouts along the east coast and other events such as the Ebola outbreaks in Africa. We need a decision from you on whether to inform the public of our enemy namely the alien presence on earth. This morning during a meeting with my division chiefs we came to the conclusion that it is time we did inform the public of the alien presence. The high frequency of attacks on our civilisation suggests to us that the aliens are about to launch a full-scale war. We have two options to discuss should you wish to inform the public," Paul Henderson Director of the CIA said.

"Oh, what are the options?" the president asked intently.

"Should you wish to inform the public then the first option would be for you to make an announcement to the nation or we can leak the information to the media," Paul Henderson replied.

"Why now?" Felix Gardner Chief of Staff asked abruptly.

"Because of the frequency of attacks not just on American soil, but around the world the aliens have been testing each country's resources, it's our conclusion that they are preparing for war. They could launch an attack today, next week or next month we are not sure, but we are confident an attack is imminent," Paul Henderson replied.

"How certain are you, because once you let the cat out of the bag then there is no going back?" Jerry Lauder Secretary of State asked incredulously.

"Yes, how certain are you of your conclusions because once we make this information public we may cause unrest and panic, which we may find difficult to control?" the president asked in a harsh tone of voice.

"All of our analysis suggests an imminent attack," Paul Henderson replied matter-of-factly.

"Okay, what is your preferred option, Paul?" the president asked calmly.

"We prefer option two where we leak information to the media," Paul Henderson replied.

"And why is that?" Felix Gardner Chief of Staff asked bluntly.

"Because half the nation believes everything the president says is fake news. Sorry, no disrespect Mr President," Paul Henderson replied.

The president looked embarrassed for a moment and his face had turned a reddish colour for all to see. He did not like being told the obvious and the truth even though he respected the opinion of the Director of the CIA. The man he had appointed to the senior position of the CIA in the early days of his presidency. The president had taken the comment personally and was having second thoughts about the Director of the CIA.

"What about our friends and allies should we inform them first before we inform the public?" the president asked with anger in his tone of voice.

"That's your decision Mr President," Paul Henderson replied curtly.

"Yes, I know, but what do you think?" the president asked bluntly.

Shrugging his shoulders Paul Henderson replied, "There will be some countries that do not know anything about the alien menace so it will be a surprise to them. Saying that...I think you should inform our friends and allies before we make anything public," Paul Henderson replied calmly.

"Well, this secret we have kept quiet about these last few years and now you want me to tell the world in an election year. You are certainly asking a lot of me and my administration. What do you think Felix and Jerry?" the president asked intently.

"Considering everything...I think we should let the CIA leak the information to the media after you have informed our friends and allies of the situation," Jerry Lauder Secretary of State replied matter-of-factly.

"And you Felix what do you think?"

"I agree with Jerry...give the responsibility to the CIA," Felix Gardner Chief of Staff replied briskly.

"Okay, when do you need a decision?" the president asked curtly.

"Now, Mr President, we need to prepare our forces," Paul Henderson replied with composure.

"Okay, I've made a decision to let the CIA take responsibility, but you do realise at some stage, regardless of what you think about my standing with the citizens of America, there may come a time when I will need to make an announcement to the public to quell any unrest in the nation," the president said succinctly.

"I understand Mr President."

"When will you release the information?" Jerry Lauder Secretary of State asked bluntly.

"Within the week when we have set up a team to handle the information flow," Paul Henderson replied calmly. Continuing, he added, "You can inform our friends and allies without delay from today."

"Is that everything?"

"Yes, that concludes my briefing," Paul Henderson replied.

On leaving the Oval Office and walking down the long corridor past sculptures and paintings of past presidents to the rear of the White House to his chauffeur-driven car, Paul Henderson wondered how the public would take the news that an alien presence did exist on earth.

***

Meanwhile, Harry Steel and Dr. Susan Ginsberg were studying police reports of vehicles that had been stolen in the local area, when they received CCTV footage of the terrorists at a local convenience store.

"Our CIA database has made a match to Miss Gina Spinlotti and the vehicle they're using," Harry Steel remarked.

"You can see Ibrahim never raises his head to avoid the cameras," Dr. Susan Ginsberg said.

"Yeah, he's clever, but Spinlotti did for a second and now we can get back on their tail," Harry suggested.

"We have their vehicle heading out of town towards the local airport according to police reports," Susan said.

"Yes, it's my guess they plan to switch vehicles somewhere at the airport. The local police are currently searching for their vehicle throughout the airport carparks," Harry remarked.

***

"Harry, they've found the vehicle in the long-stay carpark and the police are now checking the CCTV cameras to see what vehicle they are currently using," Susan said.

"Good."

"The police have identified the vehicle as a Ford, light blue SUV, which was last tracked on the main highway heading towards South Carolina. We are about three hours behind," Susan remarked.

"I've just received a police report about an old man found tied up at an abandoned coal mine. It seems that he overheard the terrorists' plans. Apparently, the terrorists are heading for Tennessee to acquire more explosives. I don't know whether to believe the information or not," Harry said.

"Why's that?"

"Well, just the route they are taking, unless they plan to visit south Tennessee via Georgia, I'm not sure until we get further tracking information on their vehicle," Harry replied.

"You think it's a ruse to put us of the trail?"

"It could be, we won't know until we get further information," Harry replied.

"Our latest police report says they have lost contact with their vehicle, which suggests they have switched vehicles again. Something must have spooked them," Susan said.

"Yeah, a ghost from the past," Harry remarked.

Chapter 18

Later that day, Harry Steel and Dr. Susan Ginsberg were heading for South Carolina hoping to receive further police reports about the terrorists. The local police had lost touch with the terrorists' vehicle just inside the border between South Carolina and North Carolina. It was envisaged that the terrorists had switched vehicles again or were hold up somewhere close to the border between North Carolina and South Carolina. Harry had received a text message from his boss requesting him to report in as soon as possible.

***

"Hello, it's Harry what's up."

"Hi, Harry, I have urgent news can you get back here as soon as possible?" Michael Kurios Director of Counter Intelligence asked.

"That's difficult, I'm right in the middle of trying to catch those terrorists here in South Carolina," Harry replied.

"Leave that to the local police and the FBI. I have urgent news that I cannot say on the phone. Leave your transport there and catch a flight back here as soon as possible, it's urgent," Michael Kurios said.

"What about Susan?"

"Bring Susan with you, is that understood?"

"Yes, I understand, but I don't like leaving an investigation just as we're about to catch the culprits," Harry replied. Harry did not like leaving in the middle of an investigation it was like painting a house and leaving the ladders and all the mess for someone else to clear away. It went against the grain and was not his mode of working.

"I understand, see you later today," Michael Kurios said and hung up the phone call.

"Our boss wants us on a flight back to Langley as soon as possible," Harry said.

"We have to leave our investigation just as we're about to apprehend the culprits that don't make sense," Susan said.

"Yeah, it doesn't make sense but it's an order," Harry said. Continuing, he added, "Let's get to the nearest airport."

***

Later that afternoon, Harry and Susan were back at the CIA headquarters at Langley, Virginia sat inside Michael Kurios" office waiting for their boss to finish his phone call.

"Sorry about that. Right, I'm also sorry about dragging you both back here on such short notice, but what I have to say could not be said over the phone. And you both need to know the truth before the truth goes public. The enemy I spoke about before is not the Chinese or another country but an alien force not terrestrial to this earth. In fact, we don't know where this alien menace comes from but they are here and we believe they are getting ready to launch a war against the world," Michael Kurios said.

"Why didn't you tell me the truth when I asked you about this before?" Harry asked in disbelief.

"I know we are friends not just work colleagues but I couldn't tell you the truth before because I was under a code of silence and have been for the past couple of years ever since we found out ourselves," Michael Kurios replied.

"So the cattle mutilations and flying saucers are real?" Susan asked in disbelief.

"Yes, Susan they are real and a constant menace," Michael Kurios replied.

"Why let me travel around the world trying to

solve cases when you already knew who the culprits were?" Harry asked.

"We had to be sure and it was not my decision to lead you on goose chase it was the director of the CIA that made that choice," Michael Kurios replied.

"I thought something wasn't quite right and that you were not telling me the complete story. What happens now that you have let the cat out of the bag?" Harry asked.

"The president has decided to let the CIA handle the responsibility of informing the public through a series of leaks by us. Over the coming weeks, we will leak information to the press and the media without the need for the president needing to make a formal announcement to the nation," Michael Kurios replied.

"So that recent east coast blackout was likely the aliens at work?" Harry asked.

"Yes, the aliens have been testing our resources not just in America but also around the world. The frequency of attacks suggests to us that they are preparing to launch a full-scale war against the world. This war could come any day now or perhaps over the coming weeks and months. We noticed the heightened frequency around three months ago, but we've been preparing our defences since we realised the truth," Michael Kurios replied.

"Are we ready for an attack?" Susan asked pensively.

"Yes, our forces have been hastily preparing for such an event without alerting the aliens!" Michael Kurios replied.

"So what happens now?"

"You both can get back to finding those terrorists and in due course filing a report," Michael Kurios replied.

***

On the drive to the airport, Harry and Susan discussed what their boss had revealed to them. Both of them came away from the meeting feeling disillusioned at what their boss had told them. Harry and Susan felt that if they had been told the truth from the beginning it would have helped them in solving their cases a lot sooner. On the flight back to South Carolina, Harry told Susan about his recent trip to stay with his sister in Boston and the paranormal phenomena he experienced while he was there. He explained that around three months ago his sister had noticed the upsurge in paranormal events and could not explain why this was happening and he wondered if there was a connection with the increased frequency of the aliens' attacks, which their boss had mentioned started around the same time.

"When we land in South Carolina I've set up a meeting with the local police chief to get the latest information on the whereabouts of the terrorists," Harry said. Continuing, he added, "Until then we can discuss what we want to."

"Do you think there's a link between the paranormal events and the frequency of attacks by the aliens or just a coincidence?" Susan asked intently.

Shrugging his shoulders, Harry replied, "I'm not sure, but a coincidence seems too convenient for an answer to the enigma. In this business coincidences are rare and usually the links are there but hard to see at first."

"Tell me about your sister you never mentioned her before," Susan said.

"I never said anything before because I like to keep family matters private, but since the startling news from our boss, I now have a new paradigm to adjust to.

And besides, the link between the two could be important to understand in the coming days. My sister is much like me and can be stubborn but extremely cuddly," Harry replied, smiling.

"Would you like another drink, sir?" the air stewardess asked.

"Susan would you like a drink and for me another JD and coke, please."

"No, not for me I'm driving when we land."

"Yes, of course."

"My sister is an anthropologist and teaches at Boston University, but her hobby and passion is the study of paranormal phenomena. Much of what I know about the paranormal is from my recent experience with my sister and her investigations. She told me she had noticed an upsurge in paranormal cases starting around three months ago and was perplexed as to why that was happening. She said that the phone had been red hot with calls with people experiencing paranormal phenomena for the first time and wondered what had caused the upsurge in cases. And the upsurge in paranormal cases was not just in Boston but all over America and the world from her research she had said. The more I think about it, the more I doubt it is a coincidence," Harry said intently.

"I'd like to meet your sister sometime."

"Perhaps the next time we're in that area I'll introduce you."

"Do you believe in the paranormal?" Susan asked curiously.

"Before tagging along with my sister to a couple of paranormal events I'd have to say no, but now I've experienced those events for myself I'd have to say yes. And now what our boss has revealed to us I have to believe in aliens and flying saucers, which previously I would have said no to that as well. My world paradigm has changed completely and now I would not be surprised to see mermaids swimming in the sea," Harry said. Continuing, he added, "What about you?"

"When I was a girl aged about twelve we lived in a two-family house in the top part of the house. We would often hear the sound of someone walking down the stairs from the attic where I had my bedroom. And the cat we had would often hide frightened under the couch as if the cat could sense something or see something. We found out that there had been a murder in the house some years before, so yes I believe there are events call them paranormal that we can't explain away through logic," Susan replied.

"While we're on the subject of strange events what can you tell me about the Prion, which my sister said came out of the blue during the 'mad cow' disease back in the eighties. Apparently, they're harder to kill than a suicidal ghost," Harry said, smiling.

"Yes, I've read about them and they're extremely dangerous, but not much research has been done as far as I know. The Prion is not a virus or a bacterium, but a type of protein, which attaches itself to other important enzymes in the body and causes those enzymes to grow misshaped. This then leads to 'mad cow' disease in cattle and Creutzfeldt-Jakob (JFD) disease in humans and a hundred per cent fatality rate and usually, once diagnosed people die within a year," Susan replied. Continuing, she added, "Why do you ask?"

"It's what someone said the other day while I was with my sister conducting her paranormal inquiry. A client brought up the subject and proposed the link between the rise in dementia cases over the last few years and the possible link with the Prion. This old man who had experienced the 'mad cow' disease had said the government, at the time, had said the Prion could lay dormant and resurface in twenty to thirty years' time, which is around now and it's possibly why dementia was now such a major killer," Harry replied.

"Do you believe that's possible?"

"Right now, I believe anything is possible."

"As far as I know not much research has been done on the subject and dementia has become the number one killer in the population overtaking cancer. If there's a causal link between the Prion and dementia then the government is responsible for the lack of research and funding on the matter. All I know and have read is that the Prion is harder to kill than any living organism, but they're not a living organism much like a virus just a set of proteins that can cause serious problems for the unfortunate soul that gets infected and resulting in death," Susan said sadly.

"So a virus isn't a living organism, is that right?" Harry asked perplexed.

"Yes, that's right, according to most scientists a virus becomes active when it attaches to a living cell and then it uses the host cell to replicate itself. In the true sense of the word, it's not a living organism like a bacterium is; it's not moving about and showing signs of life. If you looked at the virus under a microscope you would see that it's inert, but has the ability to attach itself to a living cell and use that to replicate itself and cause problems. The Prion is similar in nature it's just proteins that cause other proteins in your body or in an animal to form misshapen, which then causes encephalopathy and death," Susan replied.

"What is encephalopathy?"

"Oh, yes, it's the damage and disease to the brain."

Harry grimaced at the thought and said,

"Charming, perhaps we should change the subject and besides, we're almost about to land."

***

In the office, of the local chief of police, Harry Steel and Dr. Susan Ginsberg listened to the latest information concerning the capture of the terrorists.

"We lost touch with the terrorists shortly after they crossed over the border into South Carolina. Since then, we have been searching for any sign of the terrorists throughout the state," the chief of police said.

"How long ago since you lost touch with them?" Harry asked.

"Forty eight hours ago."

"They could be anywhere in the state by now."

"We don't think they have managed to leave the state because we have roadblocks on every road leading out of the state, which has caused serious delays for motorists. And all border forces at air and seaports are on the lookout for the terrorists. They must have switched vehicles because we have not seen their vehicle on any CCTV cameras since they crossed into South Carolina," the chief of police said.

"Have you checked for stolen vehicles within a radius of fifty miles of the border?" Harry asked.

"Yes, and more, but we have failed to come up with a lead. It's as if they just vanished into thin air," the chief of police replied.

"Well, they have to be out there somewhere," Susan muttered.

"Yeah, they have switched vehicles without leaving a trace," Harry said.

"What do you want us to do now?" the chief of police asked.

"Just keep up with the search and keep the roadblocks in place," Harry said. Continuing, he added,

"Dr Ginsberg and I will drive up to the border and begin our search there."

***

When Harry Steel and Dr. Susan Ginsberg got to the last camera to spot the terrorists' vehicle they turned around and began to methodically work out the terrorist's likely progress from there.

"On this road without turning off the next camera is over five miles away. So from the last camera to spot the vehicle and this camera here they must have either switched vehicles or have holed up somewhere. Would you agree?" Harry asked.

"They have either turned right or left from the main highway and have switched vehicles or as you say are holed up somewhere," Susan agreed.

"There are plenty of isolated farms and homes around here where that is possible and to ditch a vehicle and find another," Harry suggested.

"Harry, I've just had a text from the local police they've found a burned-out vehicle matching the terrorists' vehicle not far from here at a local forest. The police have found tyre tracks of another vehicle and are currently checking to see if these tyre tracks match any likely makes of vehicle." Susan said.

"I think we need to get over there and check it for ourselves and go from there," Harry suggested.

***

Harry and Susan saw the burned-out Ford SUV located inside the forest in a clearing close to several roads leading in all directions.

"It looks as if someone picked them up here…you can just make out the footprints of someone else or they stole another vehicle and then they came back here and torched the other vehicle. My guess is someone else picked them up here and then they used the back roads before they got onto the main highway," Harry said intently.

"Oh, yes…"

"It looks like our terrorists have become aware of our endeavours to find them and have adjusted their modus operandi," Harry said.

"Yeah, they probably felt insecure and changed tactics the bastards," Susan said.

"It's my guess, they have got off the main highways to wherever they are heading for and taken minor roads where there are no cameras to track their progress."

"Clever bastards they are and they have two days ahead of us," Susan said.

"We'll catch them no doubt about that, sooner or later they will make another mistake and that will be their undoing. Fate or whatever you want to call it will intervene and make a beeline for them. I'm never surprised when the smallest detail often unravels a case faster than a speeding bullet," Harry said philosophically.

"I didn't know you believed in fate so much," Susan said.

"I didn't until I met you," Harry said, smiling.

"Well, it's an unseen force we don't fully understand but it pervades our lives whether we like or not a bit like dark matter in the universe we know it's there but we can't see it or touch it," Susan said.

"Perhaps it's all around us and we're touching it all the time…we're just not aware of it," Harry said philosophically.

"Perhaps it's something like that," Susan muttered.

"Hmm, could be…"

"Police report suggests the tyre tracks found

were common treads on sedans, so that narrows our search a bit. If they have two days on us then it's almost certain they're holed up somewhere already."

What do you think?" Harry asked intently.

"We're now looking for a needle in a haystack and they have merged into the shadows evading our sophisticated traffic cameras until they arrived at their bolthole," Susan said.

"They could be…"

"What makes you think it's in South Carolina and not farther down the east coast?" Susan asked.

"Just the assumption that someone picked them up earlier and that person would not likely to have journeyed far from their home. Somewhere in South Carolina is my guess," Harry replied.

"Langley is checking all cameras and tracking any sedans with four occupants travelling in the state, which has led to numerous possible vehicles," Susan said.

"How many leads do we have to chase?"

"Langley has narrowed it down to sixteen."

"That's too many…there must be another way to reduce the numbers. Yes, that's it…tell Langley to concentrate on any vehicle found to be closest to where the burned-out Ford SUV was found when they started their tracking." Harry suggested.

"They have two possible suspects and their final destination. One is still heading along the east coast and the other has stopped opposite the Head Island on the east coast. There are no cameras on Head Island too small an island to need them."

"My guess is Head Island, what say you?

"Yes, it's worth a shot and the local police can stop the other vehicle and check it out," Susan said.

"Get Langley to search property records against

our terrorists' current names to see if there're any matches," Harry said.

"Yes, done."

"There are no matches found according to Langley. Perhaps, they are just renting and those records aren't currently available until after six months," Susan said.

"Do the checks anyway."

***

Later that day, Harry and Susan arrived at the small town opposite Head Island and Harry summoned the coast guard to transport them over to the island. On the journey over to the island, Harry discussed with Susan their tactics should they find the terrorists.

"Apparently, there's only a population of around two hundred on the island with a few farms and homes with many being holiday homes," Susan said.

"Susan check your handgun...I feel these terrorists won't give up without a fight."

"Shouldn't we call for backup?"

"Yes, call for backup, but have the backup ready when I give the signal, is that understood? I don't want to make the situation dangerous until I'm sure we have the terrorists cornered," Harry said.

"Copy that."

"There are no roads on the island just dirt tracks for ATVs to get around. Have Langley do a search for anyone with a past criminal record and tell me what shows up," Harry suggested.

"Copy that."

"There's one name with a string of offences that lives on the west side of the island on a small farm holding."

"Steer for that," Harry said to the coast guard captain.

Within minutes, the coast guard vessel pulled along a small wooden jetty where they saw a small boat with an outboard motor tied up to the jetty.

"This looks promising."

"Copy that."

"I can see a house beyond those trees in the distance," Harry said. Continuing, he added, "Let's creep up and see if we can spot any of the terrorists."

As Harry and Susan slowly crept up to the house to the closest they could go without losing cover they waited to see signs of life in the house. Harry's instinct told him this was the terrorists' hideout. He wanted to capture the terrorists if he could without the spilling of blood. He wanted to know the terrorists' motives for future reference. Lying low behind a fallen tree they waited patiently.

"We could just call for back-up and raid the place," Susan suggested.

"Yes, I know, but let's wait for a little longer and see."

"It'll be dark in an hour," Susan muttered.

"Wait...I see someone at the window near the front door on the left can you see?"

"Yes, it's Miss Gina Spinlotti, then we're at the right place," Harry replied.

"What next?"

"Call for backup and surround the place. Ask the police to be as careful as they can be, we don't want to spook them if we can avoid it," Harry suggested.

"Copy that."

"We'll wait until the police have the place surrounded before we make another move."

Within a half-hour the police had the place surrounded and waited for Harry to call the next move. Suddenly, gunshots came from several windows from the house and all hell broke loose. The police on a loudspeaker told the terrorists they were surrounded and told them to give up or people would die. The police then launched tear gas into the house through the windows and waited. Eventually, the terrorists came out of the house with their hands in the air trying hard to breathe. The terrorists were then taken to the local police headquarters to be interviewed and formally charged.

***

"Right Ibrahim, tell us what your motivation was to start your bombing campaign," Harry asked.

"No comment."

"Look, Mr Ibrahim, you can say what you want to us, we're from the CIA and not the police," Harry said.

"No comment."

"Yes, what you tell us will not be used against you, we just need to know what made you want to start your bombing campaign," Susan said.

"No comment."

"Your comrades have already started to spill the beans about you," Harry said.

"No comment."

"Yeah, your girlfriend Sonia has told us a lot about you," Susan said.

"She doesn't know anything worthwhile about me," Ibrahim muttered.

"Okay, why don't you tell us your side of the story?" Harry asked again.

"It started when I joined a far-right group in Nebraska around ten years ago. I started attending meetings and listening to speakers who were dead against any oil pipelines crossing the state. After a period of time, I started to get like them all angry inside and I wanted to do something about the issue. Over the years the group never did anything but protest and I got disillusioned with the group and never went back to the group," Ibrahim said.

"What was the name of the far-right group you originally joined?" Susan asked.

"The Nebraska Freedom Fighters group," Ibrahim replied.

"What was it about the oil pipelines that you objected against?"

Shrugging his shoulders, Ibrahim said, "I don't know, I just got angry and the rest is history."

"What do you mean?" Harry pressed.

"I just got it in my head that I needed to do something that's all," Ibrahim replied.

"So it wasn't anything to do with Muslim extremism?" Susan asked.

"No, I was just following my anger to a logical conclusion," Ibrahim replied.

"Are there any unexploded bombs anywhere?" Harry asked intently.

"No, there isn't."

"What about Tennessee?"

"That was just a ruse to muddy the waters and send you guys in the wrong direction," Ibrahim replied.

"So, there are no explosives waiting for you in Tennessee?" Susan asked.

"None, it was just a ruse," Ibrahim replied.

"Why did you bomb the power station near Boston?" Harry asked.

"I'm not sure, it just came into my head and I followed my thoughts. It was as if someone else was guiding me. The devil inside me took over and I was then committed. To be honest, I felt like I was being controlled by an external force. I can't explain it but it wasn't me. Did the power station avert a disaster?" Ibrahim asked.

"Yes, just about."

"Good, I wouldn't want to be responsible for an ecological disaster."

"You raised the stakes after you accidentally killed that oil pipeline worker," Harry stated.

"Yeah, I didn't mean to do that…it was unfortunate. All I meant to do was destroy part of the oil pipeline, that's all," Ibrahim said.

"Okay, that just about wraps it up for now," Harry said.

"What happens now?" Ibrahim asked.

"The FBI and the police will handle your case," Harry replied.

***

Later that day, Harry filed a report and sent it to his boss before Harry and Susan boarded a flight back to Langley, Virginia. On the flight back to CIA headquarters Harry and Susan discussed recent events. Susan told Harry that after her debriefing she would be heading back to her job in Nebraska and their relationship would have to go on hold until they figured out together what they would do.

"Before you head back to Nebraska, I would like to introduce you to my sister in Boston," Harry said.

"That would be nice."

"Good, I'll send my sister a text message and let her know we're coming to see her tomorrow," Harry said.

"What about tonight?"

"We'll stay at my cabin in the Appalachians for the night before we head out for Boston," Harry replied.

"Good, changing the subject, what do you think about what our boss told us about our new enemy?" Susan asked.

"Would you like a drink, madam?" the aeroplane

stewardess asked.

"Yes, please a gin and tonic for me."

"And you sir, what would you like?"

"A JD and coke for me, thank you," Harry replied.

"I just hope our boss has got the facts correct and we can match our enemy should they attack us. If they're right about the frequency of attacks that it pertains to an all-out attack on us we should see it coming. This is all a new paradigm for you, me, and the rest of the world and it would seem our enemy has been observing us for perhaps thousands of years. You've heard about the "ancient astronaut theory," which surmises that our ancestor's thousands of years ago had help from our new enemy. It would seem they have been moulding our civilisation for someone's benefit; it is just a question of them or us. I have a lot of questions that need answers, what about you?" Harry asked.

"Yeah, much the same, if our enemy has been observing and moulding our civilisation for what purpose?" Susan replied.

"Your guess is as good as mine. If it is an experiment then it's a long-lasting one. I did read somewhere that aluminium is one of the rarest elements in the universe, yet, we use it on earth like no tomorrow because it's so abundant on this planet. Perhaps, they need our resources because they haven't felt the need to talk to us, which signals to me they have ulterior motives," Harry said.

"I don't like the idea of being someone's slave and the sooner we find out what they're up to the better," Susan said.

***

Later that day, Harry Steel and Dr. Susan Ginsberg were sat inside the office of their boss Michael

Kurios Director of Counter Intelligence at the headquarters of the CIA in Langley, Virginia and being debriefed over their recent mission to catch the Nebraska bombers.

"You've read my report?" Harry asked.

"Yes, I've read both your reports, but I would like a verbal brief from either one of you?" Michael Kurios asked.

"Okay, we were able to catch the bombers from intelligence gathered here and some guesswork on my part, which led us to their bolthole on Head Island, South Carolina. After an initial exchange of gunfire between the bombers and the police, the bombers surrendered after tear gas was used to smoke the terrorists out. We interviewed Ibrahim the lead terrorist before the FBI and the police took over the case to find out his motives and that of his associates. He regretted the attack on the power station and was glad an ecological disaster was averted by the authorities. He said he felt controlled by an unseen force and that it was not him that was controlling his mind," Harry replied.

"Well that will all come out in the wash later in the court case," Michael Kurios said. Continuing, he added, "In the meantime, have you heard the latest news about our enemy?"

"No, what's that?"

"Some in the media have read our leaks and are puzzled by our frankness and have decided the CIA is just playing a game. The media have referred to the aliens as "little green men" and are having a field day with our leaks to the public on the subject. We're having a hard time convincing them that it's the truth about the presence of aliens on our planet. The public is split right down the middle on what to believe, which was to be expected, but so far no panic which is good," Michael

Kurios said.

"What about me, sir?" Susan asked.

"I want you and Harry to finalise a report on the power station, so you'll need to head back to Boston as soon as," Michael Kurios said.

"Okay, copy that."

"Susan, you can head back to Nebraska when you have finished with the power station report. Harry, you can return here and present a verbal summary of the report before being reassigned, is that understood?" Michael Kurios asked.

"Yes, sir copy that."

***

Later that day, Harry and Susan drove to Harry's cabin in the Appalachian Mountains to spend the night together before heading out the following morning to the Boston power station. The previous night they had discussed their future together but had not finalised any future plans.

***

On arriving at the power station they were met by the director of operations. The director of operations told Harry and Susan that the power station was nearly back to normal and construction work had already begun to rebuild the pump house and the nuclear reactor was currently stable and currently being wound down. He explained to Harry and Susan that the power station would be offline for at least the next six months while this work was carried out. He explained that other power stations up and down the east coast would have to cover the loss of electricity generation and the increased demand while the power station was out of action. This could lead to further power outages, which would depend on circumstances such as load distribution across the east coast grid. The director of operations also told

Harry and Susan about the perilous state of the electricity grid and that the grid needed updating to meet the needs of the population along the east coast. He said that much of the electricity grid was outdated and needed urgent improvements to manage the expected increase in demand by the switch to electric cars. The director of operations also mentioned further sightings of strange lights seen over the power station on several occasions since the last power outage, which saw the blackout of much of the east coast.

"Have your workforce experienced any problems that may suggest interference from these strange lights seen over the power station?" Harry asked intently. Harry wanted to know if the new enemy were still manipulating events regarding the operation of the nuclear power station.

Shrugging his shoulders, the director of operations replied, "None as far as I know, but I've heard the latest news about what the government thinks on the subject and I'm now wiser to what may be happening. It's a new paradigm shift for me and I guess for most of the workforce here."

"You and I and the whole world it would seem," Harry said.

"Did you know the truth from the beginning?" the director of operations asked.

"The short answer is no," Harry replied sternly.

"What happens now?" the director of operations asked.

"You continue with your plans and we go away and write a report for our boss," Harry said matter-of-factly. Continuing, he added, "Can I see who made the report of the recent strange lights seen over the power station?"

"Yes, it was the same guys you interviewed

before…Bob and Bill… they are currently working inside the maintenance room," the director of operations said.

***

Inside the maintenance room, Harry and Susan soon found the two maintenance workers busily working in a corner of the room.

"Hello, again just a few questions about the strange lights you reported recently." Continuing, he added, "Were the lights similar in shape and size that you had seen previously?"

"Yes, they were and now we know what the government has been hiding from us all these years," the maintenance worker said, smiling.

"How long did they appear over the power station?" Harry asked.

"Around ten minutes before they just disappeared," the other maintenance worker replied.

"Yes, that's right."

"Did you have any problems that night with any of the power station's equipment?" Harry asked.

"None, as far as we are aware of," the maintenance worker replied.

"But from now on we will know who to blame," the other maintenance worker replied, smiling.

"Yeah, you could be right," Susan muttered.

"Right that concludes what we need and thanks again for your help, Harry said. Continuing, he added, "Susan, let's get back and write our report."

"Copy that."

"I plan to make a detour and visit my sister," Harry said cheerfully.

"Does she know we're coming to see her?"

"She will soon I'll send her a text message, I'll write the report later when we're at my sister's place."

"It all sounds good to me. I look forward to meeting your sister, Harry," Susan said, smiling.

Chapter 19

Later that afternoon, at Harry sister's home in Boston, Harry, Susan and Rebecca were sat around the kitchen table discussing the recent revelations the CIA had made about the presence of an alien force on the planet and how that may affect their future plans.

"Well, what are your plans for the future together?" Rebecca asked.

"We've not fully discussed our plans still early days," Harry replied.

"Yes, that's right we're still stoking the fire," Susan replied, smiling.

"Susan plans to return to her post in Nebraska for now and I plan to sit on the fence until I decide what's best to do," Harry said. Harry had thought about retirement but did not want to make an announcement until he felt sure it was what he wanted.

"Changing the subject, have you read the DNA report, which I sent you recently?" Rebecca asked.

"Yes, it would seem we have a mystery to solve, but knowing what I know now I'm not surprised by the results," Harry replied, smiling.

"What was that?" Susan asked.

"On a recent paranormal enquiry a colleague of mine was attacked by an unseen entity and he suffered deep cuts to his back. It was as if he was attacked by something with a three-prong fork to his back. We had samples taken to check the DNA and they showed not a known living organism from this planet had attacked him. We had the DNA tested at three different laboratories and they all came back with the same results," Rebecca replied.

"And what were the results?" Susan asked intently.

"The results from three different laboratories showed that Raymond was attacked by an entity not known to this earth," Rebecca replied.

"Do you still have the keys to that bungalow?" Harry asked briskly.

"Why, do you ask?"

"I want to find out when they plan to go to war with us? Now, that I know from the DNA results that we're dealing with an alien force and not from a spiritual force then there isn't any need for a priest. If we can catch the alien entity then so it will be. I will inform my boss of the situation when I'm sure the alien entity is still around," Harry replied.

"I'm coming!"

"Yes, of course!"

"What about back-up," Susan asked.

"Have backup put on standby, until we're sure it's still there, I don't want to spook the spooks," Harry replied, smiling.

"Copy that."

Harry wondered why the alien was living in the empty building in the first place; it did not fit with his way of thinking. It may have been injured and was waiting to be picked up by its kind. He was not sure, he said to himself.

Later that evening, Harry, Susan and Rebecca made their way over to the old port district of Boston. As they parked outside the bungalow's driveway the building looked eerily spooky. The shadow of a nearby willow tree added to the darkness of the place and only the light cast from the nearby streetlamp aided their approach. They heard only the sound of dead leaves being swirled relentlessly around the ground and the willow tree branches swaying in the wind. As they entered the property Harry headed straight for the room at the end of the hallway where Raymond had been attacked. He slowly approached the door.

"Stand back!" Harry demanded.

"What's that smell? It smells like bad eggs…like sulphur," Susan said.

"Yeah, I can smell it…it stinks whatever it is," Harry stated before approaching the room Raymond had been attacked in.

He had one hand on his gun and one hand on the door handle and did not know what to expect. He carefully opened the door and with his torchlight made his way around the room. He could only see some boxes in the corner of the room and some tools that were strewn across the floor. Suddenly, Harry was tossed up in the air like confetti and thrown against the wall with such force and power that, for a moment, he almost lost consciousness. Harry soon sat up and gained his composure and looked around the room for the alien. He could not see what had attacked him, but he knew it was somewhere in the room. And for the first time he felt his mind was being controlled somehow, he said to himself.

"Are you okay Harry?" Rebecca screamed out.

"Are you alright Harry?" Susan asked.

"Did you see it?" Harry shouted back.

"No."

"Where is it?" Harry howled. He was looking everywhere but could not see anything at first.

"I can't see anything," Susan replied.

"Nor can I," Rebecca shouted back.

"Don't come in the room…stay in the hallway, I don't know what this thing will do," Harry demanded. He was not willing to risk the lives of his sister and Susan on account of his endeavours.

"Copy that."

"Wait!" Harry could see something in the corner

of the room.

"It's behind those boxes!" Susan shouted as Harry saw the creature's face for the first time. And for the first time, an incredible dread ran through his body like an ill chill on a cold night. He did not know what to expect next.

"Keep your distance and your gun ready!" Harry shouted.

"Copy that."

"Be careful, Harry!" Rebecca shouted. She had seen what the alien was capable of when it had attacked her colleague Raymond and was worried for her brother.

"Come out!" Harry demanded as the creature appeared above the boxes. His first impression of the alien was that it was a hideous creature just like the reports he had read about the "greys" as they were sometimes referred to. The smell was acrid. As the creature stepped into the torchlight Harry could see it had an oversized head compared to its body and springily legs and arms. It had large almond shape eyes and no discernible ears and nose and with only what appeared to be a small slit for a mouth that he could see. It also appeared to be wearing some sort of grey colour space suit over most of its body. Harry noticed the alien had only four fingers and four toes and was around three foot tall. Harry wondered if the creature could understand him, he said to himself.

"I want to talk. Do you understand me?" Harry asked.

Suddenly, the alien stepped forward into the full glare of the torchlight. Harry felt the alien communicating through his mind and in his language.

"I look hideous to you and you to me," the alien said.

"I didn't know what to expect, but, yes, you look

like a typical 'grey' alien as so many people have described your kind," Harry said out loud.

"Are you talking to the alien?" Susan asked.

"Yes, it's communicating through my mind," Harry replied.

"So, what do you want?" the alien asked.

"When do you plan to attack us?" Harry howled.

Again, Harry felt the communication through his mind and the alien said, "When the experiment ends the war will begin."

Harry grimaced and said, "Experiment, what experiment?"

"Harry, has it told you when the war will begin?" Susan asked.

"Yes, it says when the experiment ends the war will begin! It's communicating through my mind again," Harry replied.

Harry grimaced again and said, "What experiment?"

Harry again felt the message in his mind and the alien replied, "My master's experiments on this planet. You have noticed these experiments, when the experiments have finished then the war will begin."

"I want you to come with us!" Harry suggested and was immediately thrown back against the wall.

"Call for back-up, Susan."

"Copy that."

"I either walk out of here free or you will have to kill me, either does not matter you will not stop the experiments," the alien said through Harry's mind again.

"Get ready to blow this mother fucker to hell," Harry said.

"Copy that."

"Don't you realise you have been the experiment? From the moment, you were born and for every other living organism on this planet you call earth we have been shaping your futures. At certain times, the DNA of your species and the millions of other organisms on this planet has been altered to suit our needs. You are not a product of Darwinian evolution but a product of our experiments," the alien replied.

"What are your needs?" Harry asked.

"Isn't obvious, your resources," the alien replied.

"When will the war begin? Harry asked again. He was eager to extract as much information as he could if he could not capture the alien.

"I told you when the experiment ends the war will begin," the alien said through Harry's mind again.

"How long have you been on this planet?" Harry asked.

"For many thousands of years," the alien said.

"The alien says they have been here for thousands of years and that our lives are just a product of an experiment. We are the experiments. That's what the alien says," Harry said.

"If you kill me it will not change anything?"

"What resources do you need?"

"If you fire your gun you will die with your friends," the alien said forcibly through Harry's mind.

"Harry, backup has surrounded the property," Susan said.

"Have them stand-by until I signal, is that understood?"

"Copy that."

Harry now had a dilemma; he did not want to risk the lives of his sister and Susan on trying to stop the alien from leaving.

"What resources do you want?" Harry asked again.

"Everything, especially, the metal you call

aluminium, which is always used in the making of special alloys for our spacecraft and the spacesuits we wear. Your planet has an abundance of aluminium, whereas in the universe it is very rare. It is only produced when a certain size star goes supernova and explodes. It is a very rare event in the galaxy," the alien said.

"Why have you waited so long?"

"For all experiments to converge to the singularity," the alien said through Harry's mind.

"What singularity?"

"What my masters' command," the alien said.

"Who are your masters?" Harry asked. He wanted to know as much as possible about the alien entity before it disappeared.

"My masters sent us here long ago to find resources for our planet. My masters are many and are the supreme beings on our planet we call Patanuee. My masters made us so we could travel throughout the universe to collect the information they require," the alien said.

"It says they have many masters and were sent here to collect information. It says they come from a planet called Patanuee," Harry said.

"Ask it why it is here in this house?" Susan suggested.

"Why are you here in this house?"

"It was empty and I could wait to be picked up later by spacecraft," the alien said.

"The alien says the house was empty and it was waiting to be picked up by spacecraft," Harry said out loud.

"Oh, ask the alien why it attacked Raymond?" Rebecca asked.

"Why did you attack our friend?"

"It is standard procedure," the alien replied.

"What were you doing here?"

"Observing the rail terminal," the alien said.

"Okay…"

"If you use that gun you and your friends will die," the alien said through Harry's mind again.

At that moment, Harry looked across to his sister and Susan standing in the hallway and winced at the thought of risking their lives in the capture of the alien. The CIA would have to understand the situation, he was faced with, he said to himself. And if they did not, then he was ready to retire from the CIA without regret.

At times, the sounds of the raging storm outside of the wind and rain peppered the windows like a restless soul knocking on the windows for attention. Outside the house, the cops were getting restless and wet waiting for Harry's signal to come.

"When does your spacecraft come to pick you up?" Harry asked.

"I do not know, from whence it came," the alien replied.

"I cannot let you go, you understand?"

Suddenly, Harry was thrown against the wall again with such ease as if he was a toy doll that he was like putty in the hands of the alien. He could not do anything to stop it, he was powerless. He still had his gun in his hand but he was not willing to die for a needless cause as trying to capture the alien. He would work out a scenario where the alien went free, he said to himself.

"Okay, stop it!" Harry howled and put his gun back in its holster.

"Put your gun back in its holster Susan," Harry said with a worried tone of voice. He was not sure what the alien would do next and wanted to protect Susan and his sister if he could.

"What?"

"You heard me…put your gun away, now!" Harry demanded. Susan quickly put her gun back in its holster as Harry had requested. She gazed at Harry with a look of worry on her face and wondered what Harry was going to do next. The thought of letting the alien go free would go against CIA procedures and Harry would have to do a lot of explaining at the debriefing at Langley headquarters when he gave their boss the report of this incident.

"Request backup to stand down and disperse, understood?" Harry demanded. He was not sure it was the right move at that moment, but it made sense to him, he said to himself.

"Copy that."

"Listen, we're letting the alien go free. And we walk out of here alive. That's the deal. Is that understood?" Harry said.

"Copy that."

"Don't make any sudden moves. Move back and give the alien some space."

"We're making a strategic withdrawal," Harry said.

***

"Hello, it's Harry. I have an alien needing our assistance."

"What are you talking about?" Michael Kurios asked.

"I know why they are here."

"What?"

"The alien force you told me about, we had one surrounded, but I had to let it go."

"Why didn't you inform me before of this?" Michael Kurios said with a sharp tone of voice. He then winced at the thought of not being informed about such an important event.

"I did...I sent a text message."

"Sorry! I'm reading it, now!" Michael Kurios replied.

"Good!"

"Whatever you have to say...it can wait until tomorrow," Michael Kurios said and hung up.

Harry was not sure what his boss would say about his actions concerning the alien, but he felt confident that he had made the right choice under the circumstances. He was not about to risk the lives of his sister and Susan for the sake of the kudos of capturing an alien. Regardless of CIA procedures, he felt he had no other choice, but to let the alien go free.

Chapter 20

On the drive, back to Langley, Virginia, it was raining heavily as Harry coasted along the road in his car. He had taken Susan to Boston airport and felt immediately empty without Susan around. He had a lot to think about, not least what he would say to his boss. The alien fiasco was behind him now and all that mattered was ahead of him, he said to himself. He felt that if the CIA and his boss could not understand his reasons for letting the alien go then he would be willing to retire without any regrets.

As Harry stood in front of his boss's desk and waited for him to finish his phone call, he wondered what his boss would make of his actions concerning the alien.

"Okay, give me a report of your actions in Boston," Michael Kurios said.

"Both the power station and the alien you want?" Harry asked.

"No, I can read your report of the power station later. I just want a verbal report about the alien incident," Michael Kurios replied.

"I told you before about my holiday with my sister and her passion for the paranormal. Well, on a visit to an empty house where a colleague of my sister got attacked by an unseen force causing deep wounds to his back. After having three different laboratories run DNA analysis on the wounds the results showed that the attack came from not a living organism on this planet. The attack came from an alien force and not from a spiritual force. So, I convinced my sister and Susan that we should go back to the house and ascertain whether the alien force was still present in the house. I wanted to see if I could find out crucial information regarding when the alien force would start their war against us.

"And did you?" Michael Kurios asked.

"After it eventually revealed itself in a physical form, which it conformed to the description of the 'greys' that I have read about, I then started to interrogate the alien. It told me that they have been conducting experiments for thousands of years on earth and at certain times they have been manipulating our DNA and that of other animals and organisms," Harry said.

"This alien spoke to you?" Michael Kurios asked.

"Yes, through my mind it would answer questions," Harry replied.

"What else did you find out?" Michael Kurios asked.

"The alien said the war would begin when the experiments had finished and this would be when their masters had achieved a singularity," Harry replied.

"What does that mean?" Michael Kurios asked.

"It didn't say…only when the experiments had finished would the war begin. The alien had repeated its message. I asked why they were here. The alien said they were here for our resources such as aluminium, which it said was very rare in the galaxy and they needed to use it as an alloy to make their spacecraft and the spacesuits they wear," Harry replied.

"What else did it tell you?" Michael Kurios asked.

"It said you could not stop the experiments. I drew my gun on the alien and was tossed around the room from an invisible force several times until I put my gun back in its holster. I also told Susan to put her gun back in its holster who was standing in the hallway with my sister. The alien said that I would die along with my sister and Susan if I didn't allow the alien to go free. I had to make a judgement and decided the risk was too high to risk trying to capture the alien. So, I made a tactical retreat from the house and called off the backup and issued a stand-down order," Harry replied.

"What was the alien doing in that property?" Michael Kurios asked.

"It said the house was empty and it was checking on the local railroad terminal. It also said it was waiting to be picked up by spacecraft. I have the place under surveillance twenty-four-seven by CIA operatives with explicit instructions just to watch the house," Harry replied.

"Did you ask about the frequency of attacks?" Michael Kurios asked.

"Yes, the alien did not answer, but just repeated the war would begin when the experiments had finished," Harry replied.

"So, you let the alien go free," Michael Kurios said.

"Yes, I told you…every time I mentioned capture the alien used an invisible force to toss me around the room as if I was a toy doll to throw around with ease. The alien said if I tried to capture or stop it from going free it would kill all three of us and I could not take that risk. So, in the end, I made a tactical retreat and let the alien go free," Harry said

"So, what did you really learn from the alien and can the information be relied on?" Michael Kurios asked.

"Well, we know now what they want and when the war will begin," Harry replied.

"Pity, we couldn't capture the alien for further interrogation and I understand your situation at the time. The alien said they had been here for thousands of years, but why so long?" Michael Kurios asked.

"I don't know, only that they had been manipulating our DNA to suit their needs over the time they have been here. The alien said our planet was very rare in the galaxy because of its abundance of aluminium, which only occurs in the galaxy when a certain size star goes supernova and explodes and this is when aluminium is produced. It said without aluminium they could not make the alloys needed for their spacecraft and their spacesuits," Harry replied.

"And what was the singularity?" Michael Kurios asked.

"I'm not sure the alien just said when the experiments had reached a singularity then the war would begin. The alien said we would know when that happens," Harry replied.

"Was there anything else the alien said?" Michael Kurios said.

"No, I don't believe so...I have covered everything," Harry replied.

"Well, I will take your report to the director and we will see what he wants to do. You may get reprimanded for going against CIA procedures, do you understand?" Michael Kurios asked.

"No, I don't understand, because I did what any other sane person would do in the circumstances. If you expected me to risk the lives of other people as well as my own just to capture an alien then you need to change the CIA procedures," Harry said intently.

"Look Harry it was procedure and you didn't follow it," Michael Kurios said sharply.

"I did everything possible to capture the alien, but I wasn't prepared to go on a suicide mission against overwhelming odds. I joined the CIA to serve my country and not to risk the lives of innocent people,"

Harry said intently.

"It wasn't your decision to make only to obey orders and follow procedures," Michael Kurios said.

"What would've you done in similar circumstances?" Harry asked.

"That's not the issue here, I'm not responsible," Michael Kurios replied.

Shrugging his shoulders, Harry said, "Perhaps, our friendship has ended. You seem to care more about procedures than my life and the lives of innocent people."

"You don't know that…the alien may have been bluffing," Michael Kurios said.

"Sorry, I didn't realise it was a poker game to you," Harry said angrily.

Michael grimaced at the words from Harry and said, "Look, I'm your boss and you didn't follow protocols. It's as simple as that. Fucking hell, Harry get real."

"Get real, how real you want me to get…dead for what purpose but some outdated CIA procedures so you can have the kudos of announcing to your fellow directors that you have captured an alien. What planet are you from? There was no way to capture the alien without killing it and in the process killing me and other innocent people," Harry said.

"You don't know that," Michael Kurios said.

"You weren't there…the alien threw me about without touching me as if I was a softball to play with. The threat was real. I made a decision that saved lives against an enemy we have never encountered before with such a deadly force," Harry said angrily.

"Calm down!"

Harry shook his head in disbelief and said, "You just don't get it and perhaps you will never understand."

"I understand your reasons, but you didn't follow protocols and you could've allowed the police to arrest the alien, instead, you stood down the police against standard protocols," Michael Kurios said.

"How many police officers would you like to have seen dead from your folly?" Harry asked rhetorically.

"That's not the point!"

"Yes, it is because you would have had a massacre on our hands if I had followed your advice."

"You don't know that."

"I made a decision and the right one!"

"Perhaps you did and we will never know. In the meantime, just calm down! Whatever happens…happens. We shall see what the director thinks on the matter. I will cover your back as a friend and as your boss," Michael Kurios said calmly.

"Yes, I understand," Harry replied. Harry knew that sometimes you were hailed as a hero and next a villain, it was all part and parcel of the job. In his mind he did not care, he knew he had made the right decisions to let the alien go free. If the CIA wanted to impose sanctions on him then he was prepared to walk away and start a new life somewhere else. He was always being told that he was not irreplaceable, which he knew was true for everyone in the agency no matter what rank. The thought of early retirement had crossed his mind several times since meeting Susan and he planned to discuss this with her the next time they talked together. In Harry's mind, fate had laid out another bridge to cross, which was a decision he had to take, he said to himself.

"Okay, leave it with me and we will see what happens," Michael Kurios said.

"In the meantime, what do you want me to do?" Harry asked.

"I suggest you stay here and finalise some of your previous cases and wait to hear from me. We will see want the director wants to do with you," Michael Kurios replied.

Harry shrugged his shoulders and said, "Okay!"

On the walk down to his office on the first floor, Harry wondered what the outcome would be, but was not worried. He had already decided in his mind what he would do if the outcome was not to his liking. He would apply for early retirement and seek out other pursuits. What those pursuits would be, he was not sure, he said to himself.

Sat with a coffee in his office he started to think about his future with Susan and the prospect of buying a boat and spending time cruising around the Florida Keys. He did not immediately need to find another job to pay the bills because he had saved plenty of money over the years to tide him over. There were many ideas bouncing about in his head, but most of all he wanted to be with Susan. If she wanted to continue with her career in the CIA then that would be alright as well. The prospect of living in Nebraska he could get used to and was sure fate would find a new role for him wherever he ended up living at.

Late that day, at his home in Washington D.C. Harry was busy researching the Prion, which he felt he needed to do. He wondered why governments had not spent the money researching the possible links with dementia and other brain diseases. The British government had buried the evidence in pits and forgotten about the menace for twenty years hoping it would never resurface again. Harry felt it was a fool's error trying to hide the truth. Perhaps there had been a conspiracy at the time and the government were just playing with people's lives or had it been the work of the alien force, he said to himself.

***

"Hi, Susan how are you?"

"I've missed you the moment we parted. My friends and colleagues at work wondered what had happened to me. I had to make up a story!" Susan replied.

"I hope it was a good story!"

"Ummm, it needed to be."

"I'm planning to fly out to see you at the weekend if I can. It depends on what happens here. Our boss didn't take my reasons for not capturing the alien too kindly. But, I told him, I made the right decisions given the circumstances." Harry said.

"Well, the CIA is like that… they only care about results but forget that we're human as well," Susan remarked.

"Yeah, I know what you mean."

"Where are you now?"

"At home in D.C."

"Love you!"

"I'll ring tomorrow…to finalise my plans…love you!" Harry said before ending the call.

***

Later that evening, Harry was busy again researching the Prion on the Internet. He just did not believe in coincidences and it was bugging him since old man Tiller had mentioned his experience with the 'mad cow' disease fiasco back in the late eighties. He was learning what he could on the subject and trying to understand what government and commercial research had been done on the Prion.

Chapter 21

Harry was also busy trying to find out what the "singularity" meant. The alien had not explained what the "singularity" was and he and the CIA were perplexed at what it could mean. He had the boys and girls in the basement of the CIA headquarters busily using the full resources of the CIA computers trying to find an answer.

"So tell me what you have found out?" Harry asked intently.

"According to our research, the 'singularity' is any point in time when the laws of physics break down and the outcome cannot be predicted. It's a lot more complicated than that but that's the nuts and bolts of the matter," Jamie said at the CIA headquarters basement computer centre.

"Give me some examples," Harry suggested.

"A classic example would be a 'black hole' where at the centre all known laws break down and space and time are no longer relevant and cannot be predicted. Another example would be a 'technological singularity,' which predicts a point in time when computer intelligence has advanced to such an extent that it cannot be reversed and again the results are unpredictable. Another example is a mathematical function where a given function doesn't have a defined means of behaviour beyond our present understanding of that function," Jamie said.

"So what is your best guess at what the alien was trying to describe?" Harry asked intently.

"That's a difficult question to answer. I wouldn't want you to go away with the wrong idea. Another example of a singularity would be the existence of God although I cannot prove that," Jamie replied. His background as an African American and being brought up within the Christian Church perhaps shaped his view, he said to himself.

"I didn't realise you were religious?" Harry asked.

"I don't think there's just nothing as the "big bang" theory of how the universe started, but that's my view," Jamie replied.

"You didn't answer my question, Jamie."

"Your guess is as good as mine, but if I was taking a shot at the problem then I would say a 'technological singularity' that would be my guess. But, remember it's only a guess," Jamie said.

"I guess the head honchos will form a committee to figure out what the alien meant by a 'singularity' and then formulate a response," Harry remarked.

"Is there anything else you want me to research?" Jamie asked intently.

"Yes, find out what research has taken place into the Prion. It came to the world's attention in the late eighties and was associated with the 'mad cow' disease at that time," Harry replied.

"Is this a case you are currently working on?" Jamie asked curiously.

"No, it's something that's been bugging me since I heard about it and the links it may have with dementia. Keep it to yourself and let me know what you find out as soon as possible," Harry replied.

***

Later that day, Harry Steel was stood in front of his boss inside his office on the third floor at CIA headquarters. He was waiting for his boss Michael Kurios to finish his phone call and to find out what the director of the CIA had said about his actions not to capture the alien.

"Sorry, about that Harry," Michael Kurios

Director of Counter Intelligence said. Continuing, he added, "I have good and bad news."

"Let me have the bad news first," Harry suggested, smiling.

"I thought you may say that. The bad news is that the director was not pleased with your actions to stand down the police who had the alien surrounded. He said you went against CIA procedures and possibly lost the chance for our side to gain an edge on the alien force. He understood your reasons, but you still went against procedures. So, he feels you need to be taken off active duty for a period of time until you have attended a retraining course," Michael Kurios said.

"But, he wasn't there…"

"Hold on Harry you haven't heard the good news! The director wants you to take a month-long sabbatical with full pay and then come back and take a retraining course before being put again on active duty," Michael Kurios said.

"I'll take the month-long holiday and take the reprimand on the chin," Harry said, smiling. Continuing, he added, "When does my holiday start?"

"From now, anything on your desk will be handled by other agents. I've also arranged for Dr. Susan Ginsberg to have a similar break," Michael Kurios replied.

"You know about our relationship?"

"Yes, you should know you can't hide anything within the CIA."

"Thanks for that."

"I said, I would have your back and I did. Now go and have a well-deserved holiday. Also, there is something you should know. I would have done the same thing as you did with the alien," Michael Kurios said.

"Really…"

"Yes, I would have made the same decision given the circumstances," Michael Kurios replied.

"Well, it's good to know we're still friends," Harry said.

***

Later that day, Harry Steel was on a flight to Nebraska and thinking of Susan before he fell asleep with a JD and coke in his hand. He had already phoned Susan with the news and she had already confirmed her unexpected holiday to Harry. When Harry landed at Omaha, Susan was there to greet him.

"What plans have you for our holiday together?" Susan asked.

"I thought we could hire a boat and sail down the Mississippi River and just relax and enjoy ourselves. Do you have any ideas what you would like to do?" Harry asked.

"None, just to be with you and forget about everything and everyone until our holiday is over," Susan said.

"Good, tomorrow we will drive down to the river and hire a boat," Harry suggested.

"Until then, let's just have a drink and relax."

"I've just received a text message from Jamie at Langley. He has information for me that I wanted, but I don't know if I should answer the message it may upset our plans."

"Oh, I see…"

"Hello, Jamie what have you got for me?" Harry asked impatiently.

"Plenty, it turns out very little research has been carried out into the so-called Prion. That's because at the time the British government deemed it necessary to bury the evidence and save their beef industry. They said at the time that the Prion could stay dormant for twenty to thirty years or more, but how they knew this, I haven't so far been able to find out. Anyway, it's plausible that the British government knew a lot more and decided to hide it from the public and therefore save their meat industry. I was able to find a professor who did some research into the Prion and he is still alive but retired, his name is Professor David Wilcox and lives in Lebanon, New Hampshire and his full address and phone number I have sent in a text message," Jamie said.

"Great, what else did you find out?" Harry asked briskly.

"You probably already know this…"

"Perhaps, but go ahead."

"Well, the whole saga about the 'mad cow' disease apparently occurred because someone thought it was a good idea to feed herbivores with meat from different species as well as their own. This was the story put out by the British government at the time to account for the appearance of the Prion. To me, this doesn't stack up, because the evidence is not there to prove that case. It's only a gut instinct, but something stinks rotten," Jamie said.

"I hear what you are saying and I had similar misgivings," Harry said. Continuing, he added, "Anything else I should know?"

"Yes, if it was infected feedstuff back then that travelled around the world because America and other European countries experienced the 'mad cow' saga but to a lesser extent. But, before appropriate action was taken to cull the affected animals a lot of beef was made into beef burgers. Anyone eating contaminated meat would have consumed the Prions and therefore liable to contract the human form of 'mad cow' disease. They call it Creutzfeldt - Jakob disease (CJD) in humans and it is fatal in all cases. The 'mad cow' disease in cattle is called bovine spongiform encephalopathy (BSE), which affects the nervous tissue and spinal cord and leads to degenerative brain functions. According to my research, you can get the human form of the disease only through an injection or by consuming infected nervous tissue and spinal cord. The last known case of BSE was a cow being randomly sampled at a farm in California in two thousand and twelve. What is not so clear is why and how this cow was carrying this deadly disease. The Centre for Disease Control (CDC) was insisting there was no risk to the food chain at the time, but did not mention anything about how the cow contracted the disease, which is weird, to say the least," Jamie said.

"That is weird because we're told it started with infected feedstuff, then why was it in this one cow in California?" Harry asked.

"I don't know, that's why I think you need to contact Professor David Wilcox, perhaps he can provide some answers," Jamie replied. Continuing, he added, "According to my research the Prion can stay dormant from anything between twelve to fifty years or more. So, that average of twenty years may be out of sync with current knowledge of its behaviour."

"Okay, thanks for your help and let me know as soon as possible what else you dig up, bye for now," Harry said and hung up the phone call.

"Sounds like you're getting busy again," Susan said rhetorically.

"Well, it's been bugging me since I heard about the Prion and its association with dementia and other brain disorders. Since we were told about the alien presence on earth and those cattle mutilations, I've started to put two and two together," Harry remarked.

"You're meant to be on holiday."

"Yes, we are, but something doesn't stack up and

I need to find out what it is," Harry stated. Continuing, he added, "Fancy a trip to New Hampshire?"

"I thought you said you were going to hire a boat for a trip down the Mississippi?" Susan asked curiously.

"Yes, I am but later this week if the professor will see us."

"What professor?"

"Professor David Wilcox who did some research into the Prion before he retired," Harry replied.

"Oh, okay, I like the sound of us jetting around the country," Susan said.

"We could do some sightseeing while we're in New Hampshire and spend a few days there."

"Sounds good to me, changing the subject what other plans had you in mind?" Susan asked curiously.

"Whatever you would like to do is fine with me. But, we could spend some time in Florida and get some sun, it's only an idea," Harry said sheepishly.

"No, that sounds a great idea," Susan replied. Continuing, she added, "That professor what was his field of study?"

"Jamie didn't say, I'll text Jamie and find out, I'll do it now," Harry replied.

"That was quick; Jamie says the professor is a microbiologist and studied the effects of pathogens on animals and humans before he retired," Harry said.

"The same as me, but the area of study is huge and it pays to specialise, which I did not," Susan said.

"Yes, I know you're a microbiologist, but you never specialised in any particular area. Is that true?"

"Yes, that's correct. I studied the genetics of plants because I was interested in improving crop yields, but got side-tracked and joined the CIA for my sins," Susan said flippantly.

"What sins were those?" Harry asked, smiling.

"I wanted the adrenalin rush of CIA cases because at the time I was bored with my career. But, now I have found new meaning to my work in Nebraska, which I hadn't felt before," Susan replied.

"Good, whatever you decide I'm fully okay with. I was thinking about retiring and moving out here at some point. Langley always likes to point out how you're not irreplaceable, which makes sense, but it sometimes hurts your ego. It will make a welcome change not to kill people for a living; perhaps, I could become a rancher and ride the prairie."

***

The following day, Harry and Susan had hired a boat and were happily sailing down the Mississippi River. The boat was a single mast sloop with a diesel engine. They had provisions for a couple of days and would sail by day and rest up at a town along the river during the night. It was safer that way because Harry had no experience of handling a boat nor did Susan. Harry had time to reflect on his hunch about the alien force on earth. It was like an itch you had to scratch, he said to himself.

"Hello, Professor David Wilcox my name is Harry Steel. Can I come with my partner Dr. Susan Ginsberg and interview you about your research into the Prion. Would this Friday be okay around twelve?" Harry asked.

***

The day after, Harry and Susan took a flight to Lebanon, New Hampshire and on arrival booked into a local hotel. They hired a car for the short drive to Hanover, which was close to the border with Vermont where Professor David Wilcox lived. The professor had told Harry that he lived in a remote area on the outskirts of the city of Hanover and that he would need a Satnav to find the place. As Harry and Susan drove through the forest, which seemed to surround them they eventually came upon the professor's home situated in a clearing surrounded by a forest of deciduous trees.

***

"Hi, Professor Wilcox, my name is Harry Steel and this is Dr Susan Ginsberg."

"Come in and make yourselves at home. Now, what would you like to know?" the professor asked.

"I understand that you did some research into the Prion before you retired?" Harry asked.

"Where did you say you are from?" the professor asked intently.

"We didn't, this is a private matter, but we both work for the CIA." Harry and Susan then showed their identity cards to the professor. Continuing, he added, "I've had a hunch about this for some time and needed to find out if I'm right."

"Carry on," Susan said watching on.

"Yes, I spent a number of years studying the 'mad cow' disease called BSE which stands for bovine spongiform encephalopathy and in humans Creutzfeldt-Jakob disease," the professor replied.

"What were your conclusions?" Susan asked intently.

"Well, there's the published version and the unpublished version, which would you like to hear?" the professor asked.

"Both!"

"In the published version I stuck with the facts, evidence and the data, which showed that the pathogen called the "Prion", was the culprit in both forms of the disease. It was harder to kill than any other known pathogen or living organism on the planet. The Prion was much like a virus but not a virus but a protein that could attach itself to other proteins in the living organism such as a human and force that human protein to form misshapen and therefore induce brain disorders such as dementia. It was a deadly pathogen and fatal in all cases. Tests that were done in Britain during the mid-nineties outbreak showed you needed temperatures approaching three thousand degrees to kill it. Normal cooking temperatures were insufficient to kill the pathogen and anyone eating infected meat would be exposed to the pathogen and die from the disease it caused. What was weird about the pathogen is that it could stay dormant in a human for many years anything up to fifty years before it sowed its destruction," the professor said.

"And your unpublished version," Harry said.

"As you all know as a scientist you stick with the facts, evidence and the data. Well, in my view there were anomalies that didn't stack up. At the time, the British were having a difficult time understanding how to deal with the pathogen because it literally came out of the blue. At first, they started to burn the infected cattle but soon realised all they were doing was spreading the pathogen into the surrounding area because the fires didn't kill the pathogen. Next, they chose to bury the dead animals in plastic-lined pits to avoid the chance of any pathogens leaking into the water table. We hope they were successful because if not then a lot more people could become infected in the coming years. The anomaly was the speed at which it manifested itself, literally overnight," the professor said.

"But was it not the infected feedstuff that caused the outbreak in the cattle?" Harry asked.

"Yes, that's what we were told by the way of feeding cattle with feed produced from cattle that had died from other causes. Was it the process of feeding herbivores meat that caused the pathogen to appear or was it already in the feedstuff? You have to ask the question was it a dead animal that already had the disease and was processed into feed, which was ultimately fed to healthy animals. A more likely scenario if you ask me. Now, you have to ask the question how did that animal contract the disease, did it happen by itself or was it induced?" the professor asked.

"What do you mean induced?" Harry asked intently.

"Normally, in nature, we understand how diseases manifest themselves, we're given a fair warning from how we rear animals, yet, and this did not happen and why is that? We understand how diseases jump from one species to another, but no one has found the link in the animal kingdom that may have occurred in this case. It is as though someone induced the disease to the species," the professor said.

"Is that possible?" Harry asked in disbelief.

"Yes, all it takes is a syringe with the pathogens injected into the animal's spinal cord or similar tissue. Of course, this is only conjecture, on my part, but that's why I did not publish my thoughts on the issue. Recently, the CDC found by random sampling a cow with BSE in California. Now, how did that occur because the CDC hasn't published how that happened? There could be other animals getting affected and getting into the food chain without anyone knowing about it. The problem could be huge; we just don't know." Continuing, he added, "Does that answer all your questions?"

"Yes, it does," Harry replied and Susan affirmed.

"Oh, what this I hear on the news about the truth of an alien presence on earth, is that true?" the professor asked.

"Yes, it seems so." "It wouldn't surprise me to learn the aliens have been fucking with our food supply in some experiment," the professor said.

"You could be right!" Susan said as Harry nodded his head in agreement.

***

And then one day, the experiments suddenly stopped and there were no more human abductions or cows being found mutilated or any further sightings of strange lights in the sky and the attacks by deadly viruses had stopped, but the war was about to begin. The singularity had begun. There was nowhere to hide and nowhere to run.

Ingram Content Group UK Ltd.
Milton Keynes UK
UKHW042314100723
424904UK00001B/10